Neil Zurcher's *Favorite*

ONE TANK TRIPS

& Tales from the Road

GRAY & COMPANY, PUBLISHERS
CLEVELAND

Gray & Company, Publishers
11000 Cedar Avenue
Cleveland, Ohio 44106

ISBN 1-886228-01-9
Printed in the United States of America
10 9 8 7 6 5 4 3

To my wife, Bonnie;
to my kids, Melody, Melissa, and Craig,
who traveled so many miles with me through the years;
and to the man who taught me to love Ohio:
my father, Oscar F. Zurcher (1908–1990).

Acknowledgments

I am indebted to many people who made this book possible: to WJW-TV President and General Manager Virgil Dominic, for creating the idea of One Tank Trips back in 1980 and for his many kindnesses to me; to WJW-TV News Director Grant Zalba, who has allowed me the freedom to wander where I wish each week; to all of our talented videographers and editors at WJW-TV, many of whom you will meet in this book, and who travel with me each week throughout the year; and to publisher David Gray, for convincing me it was time that this book was written.

Contents

Contents *(continued)*

Contents *(continued)*

How It All Started

IN 1967 WHEN I WENT TO WORK for WJW-TV, I discovered that I enjoyed doing feature stories—wandering the backroads of Ohio, seeking out the little stories that didn't ordinarily make the news. This was even before Charles Kuralt of CBS began his national wanderings. In fact, when Kuralt began his "On the Road" series in 1968, I did a parody of him in a half-hour documentary we called "R.F.D." I borrowed a huge converted Greyhound Scenicruiser bus from a friend, John Morse, chairman of the board of Morse Instruments in Hudson. John didn't like to fly, but he loved to travel and had converted this bus into a luxury home on wheels, with a movie theater on board as well as bedrooms, kitchen, and traveling office. It was magnificent! In a final scene I turned to the camera and said, "Charles Kuralt, eat your heart out."

We Americans have always been a pretty mobile society, at least in the twentieth century. So in 1980 when the mideast oil powers raised prices and threatened to cut back on petroleum supplies, Americans were hit with spiraling prices at the gasoline pump and, even worse, long lines waiting to buy the high-priced gasoline.

My boss at that time, then-news-director Virgil Dominic, now president and general manager of WJW-TV, was truly concerned that with summer coming many Ohioans would not be able to afford much of a vacation. He called me into his office to discuss an idea he had.

Virgil proposed that, because of my experience wandering the highways and byways of Ohio, I should do a week-long series of reports on places that people could reach for a vacation on just one tank of gasoline. He said, "Let's call it a 'one tank trip!'"

Originally, the series was just meant to be one week long. Enough to show folks that, even with gasoline shortages, there were places to go for a holiday that summer that were fun and yet close to home. But neither Virgil nor I expected the response to the series. The phones began to ring and the mail started to come in. People wanted more ideas on destinations.

Virgil sent me a memo telling me to put together a once-a-week segment for the rest of the spring and summer that would offer other places to go.

That autumn, when we ended the once-a-week segments, the mail started to flow again. Viewers didn't want the series to end. They asked for Christmas trips and activities. Again we obliged.

By the second year it was apparent that with my "one tank" formula (out and back on a tank of gasoline), I was fast running out of places to go. I went to Virgil and proposed that we extend our distance by making the destination anyplace we could reach on one tank. Even if we had to buy a second tank of gasoline to get back home, I argued, this was still, technically, a "One Tank Trip."

Virgil agreed and now, fifteen years later, the series has become the longest-running local travel segment in television history. We travel year-round to eight states and Canada and make nearly 90 trips a year. And, with the exception of special trips to Alaska and Florida, we still take just a "one tank" trip.

From My Mailbag...

Dear Neil Zurcher,

Recently you mentioned on one of your "One Tank Trips", a place To sunbathe in The nude in Tuscarawas County in The state of Ohio.

Would you be able To Tell us The whereabouts of This place? Also, is There anyplace closer To Cleveland? We would appreciate hearing from you before The weather gets much colder.

Sincerely,

Some Thoughts while Filling the Gasoline Tank

THERE IS A VERY GOOD REASON why the U.S. Postal Service came up with Zip Codes for our mailing addresses: they had to deliver mail in Ohio.

My wife, Bonnie, who keeps track and cares about such things as where I have been, points to the problem the postal service must have had delivering mail to Ohioans before the Zip Code era.

There are 296 towns and villages in Ohio that share the same, exact name with another town or village in another county. And if that is not bad enough there are 38 instances in Ohio where three towns all share the same name. Pity the poor postman who had to determine if a letter bound for Berlin, Ohio was meant to go to the Berlin down in Williams County, or the Berlin up near Sandusky in Erie County, or the Berlin down in Holmes County where all the Amish live.

Some towns' names were so popular that they just multiplied like rabbits all over Ohio. For instance, take Avondale. There's Avondale down near the Ohio River in Belmont County, and there's Avondale over near Bellefontaine. There's Avondale near Canton in Stark County, and let's not forget the Avondale near Dayton, as well as another in Muskingham County, and the one near Cincinnati. Altogether there are six Avondales in Ohio.

And it gets worse. There are eight counties in Ohio with towns named Centerville. Now they are probably all near the center of something, which probably accounts for the name, but it makes me wonder, didn't anyone in town check the post office to see if there was another Centerville before they started painting signs at the corporate limits?

That brings us to Stringtown, Ohio, probably one of the stranger names. I can only speculate on how the name originated. Perhaps the pioneers laid out the town with bits of string to show where the various lots were. Who knows? In any event, there must have been a lot of string laid out in Ohio because Bonnie has discovered a total of *ten* towns in Ohio that share the name of Stringtown.

And the postman's real nightmare was the town of Five Points. The name probably originated from the early Native American trails that intersected and became roads and places of settlement. No less than *eleven* towns, villages, and hamlets in Ohio bear the name Five Points.

What I am leading up to here is the importance of checking addresses and directions before starting out on a One Tank Trip anywhere in Ohio, unless you like to find yourself in unexpected places and meet people who haven't the foggiest idea what you're looking for. For example, say you're heading for Boston, in Summit County, to visit the Blossom Music Center, and instead you end up at Boston down in Jefferson County. You'll probably get directions to someone's orchard if you ask anyone there how to get to Blossom.

Even if you're a seasoned Ohio traveler and think you know where everything is in the state, you may find yourself, like I did once, in the wrong Georgetown late at night, looking for a motel that doesn't exist in the Georgetown you are presently visiting. It is only then that you discover there are six Georgetowns, and the one that you want is at the other end of the state. At times like these you begin to develop a real affection for the postal service's Zip Codes and curse anyone who fails to include a Zip Code in their address.

The bottom line: use your phone. Call ahead. Get up-to-date directions, ask them to send you maps. I don't care whether you are using my travel book or someone else's, all things change with time, and if you are going to invest your family's time and money in a One Tank Trip, take a moment before you go to confirm times, places, costs, and, especially, just which Five Corners it's in.

One Tank Tip #1
Call Ahead

Always call first. Hours, prices, and even locations can change without warning. If the destination is important to you, or is some distance away, be sure to call first.

Using This Book

WHEN I TRAVEL OHIO, I DON'T think of it broken into five exact sections, northeast, northwest, southeast, southwest, and central. Rather, I loosely imagine it as a fan spreading out from Cleveland. But to organize this book it was necessary to define some geographic areas. These groupings are meant to give a general idea of where the attractions are located, to make them easier to find on a map. This may mean, for example, that the town of Millersburg, in Holmes County, is listed in a grouping of trips in Central Ohio, while Berlin, which is Millersburg's next-door neighbor, is listed under Southeast Ohio. But don't be afraid to mix and match some of the trips that are located in adjoining geographical areas.

The destinations listed in this book have been chosen by me on the basis of my own experience and from letters and phone calls I have received from "One Tank Trips" viewers over the years. None of the destinations has paid a fee to be included in this book.

Lastly, this is not intended to be a technical reference work. You won't find maps or detailed directions. Instead, this book is meant to encourage you to get out and sample some new places that might be fun, intriguing, and, hopefully, educational. Remember, half the fun of travelling is discovery. So, get out your map and plan your trip.

I offer one bit of advice. When my wife and I are on our own One Tank Trip, and I suddenly find myself at the end of a dead-end road that wasn't on the map, and she says, "You're lost, aren't you?", I always reply, "I am not lost. I just don't know exactly where I am at this moment."

Happy travels.

Neil Zurcher's *Favorite*

ONE TANK TRIPS

TRIPS

& Tales From The Road

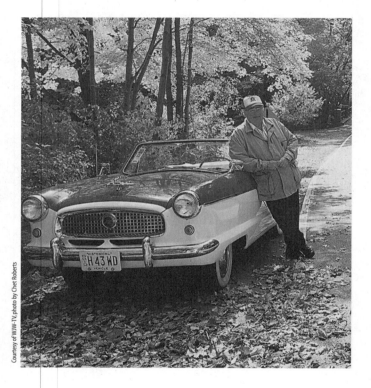

Courtesy of WJW-TV, photo by Chet Roberts

1 **What Is That Car?**

THE QUESTION I GET ASKED most often is, "What is that car you drive?"

Sometimes before I can answer somebody will pipe up and say, "It's the car Lois Lane drove in the old Superman movies." Or someone else will say, "Nahh, it's one of those kit cars, you know, like you build yourself."

They're wrong on both counts. It was not the car that Lois Lane drove. She drove a Nash Rambler, which is almost twice the size of my little car. And it is not a kit car. It was a production line car for eight years before it drove off into automobile history.

The car is a 1959 Nash Metropolitan, sometimes called the "Baby Nash." It was sold by the Nash Motor Company, which later merged with Hudson to form American Motors and even later was absorbed by the Chrysler Corporation.

The tiny Nashes were manufactured from 1954 until 1962. Probably the first truly international cars, they were built for Nash in England by the Austin Motor Company after a design by Pinin Farina of Italy. In eight years of production, fewer than 900,000 of these cars were built—compare that with the millions of cars most major car manufacturers today produce each year! There were two models: a hardtop and a convertible. Both sold for about $1,500 brand new—plus tax and title, of course.

It was a good idea—this tiny economical car—that came on the auto scene at the wrong time. In 1954 America was falling in love with big motors and even bigger tail fins. The Nash Metropolitan offered neither. It had just a 4-cylinder 1,500-cc engine that could chalk up about 30 miles to the gallon. It could carry three people in the front seat and a couple of small children in a very small rear seat.

As near as we could discover, my car started life in Florida and ended up in North Canton, Ohio where it was stored for a number of years before I bought it in 1989. It has about 72,000 miles on it, and it still has the original motor.

Do we really take it on all those trips? The answer is Yes ... and No. In the earlier years we did drive it on many of the shorter trips. But as time has gone by and the car has become a favorite with viewers, we have taken it on fewer trips in order to preserve it. When we do use it, such as on a recent trip to Kelley's Island, we take quite a bit of extra footage of me driving the car and use that in segments on longer trips, or during inclement weather. The car has become a symbol of our show. In fact, at parades and personal appearances, we have had small children come up to the car and pet it. One little girl thought it was alive and gave it a hug and kiss!

A couple of times over the years we have considered replacing the little car with another vehicle, but when we polled viewers, the answer always came back, "Keep the Metro."

So we have had it painted and put new tires on it and, maybe, this spring we'll finally get around to having the motor overhauled. We'll keep driving the little red-and-white car as long as folks keep welcoming it into their living rooms via television.

Does the car have a name? We never gave it one, but Dick Goddard refers to it as the "Neil-Mobile."

IF YOU LIKE OLD CARS

Ohio is rich in auto museums; here are some of my favorites. (I have listed a few more elsewhere in the book.)

THE BEST COLLECTION IN OHIO

This is probably one of the best collections in Ohio if not the whole United States. They have a presidential limousine used by Presidents Ford through Bush. They offer some of the best examples of the earliest cars, as well as a cross-section of the cars of the twenties and thirties and just recently have added "muscle" cars from the fifties and sixties. There is something here for every member of the family. Now if they would only add a Nash Metropolitan to the collection, it would be complete.

Western Reserve Historical Society   216-721-5722
10825 East Boulevard
Cleveland, Ohio 44106   Handicapped access: yes

A PACKARD MUSEUM

This is one of the finest privately owned museums in the state. They have taken a Packard Dealership from the 1930s and restored it— right down to the service department, where the mechanic's white coat still hangs beside his personal tool chest. They have over 75 Packards on display here from the showroom to the service department.

If you like Packards don't miss this one.

Citizens Motorcar Company　　　513-226-1917
420 South Ludlow Street
Dayton, Ohio 45402　　　Handicapped access: yes

A MOTORCYCLE MUSEUM

If you are a fan of old motorcycles this one is for you. In this tiny college town just outside of Columbus there is a museum dedicated just to motorcycles, from the earliest models with side-cars and wooden frames all the way up to some of the fastest modern bikes.

Motorcycle Museum　　　614-891-2425
33 Collegeview
Westerville, Ohio 43081　　　Handicapped access: yes

NOT REALLY A MUSEUM

This place should be a museum, but it's really a used car lot that specializes in cars from the fifties, sixties, and seventies. In fact, they always have at least 50 cars on hand and in their garage. The owner doesn't charge for looking—he just asks that you not touch and be careful while walking between the tightly parked cars. Obviously a lot of "lookers" end up buying a car.

G & H Collectibles　　　216-276-7875 or 216-276-3092
165 Spring Street
Killbuck, Ohio 44654　　Handicapped access: narrow aisles between cars

2 Elephant Trouble

"YOU'RE GONNA RIDE IN an elephant race," said Mickey Flanagan, our assignment editor.

"A WHAT?" I replied.

"An elephant race," he said with some finality as he turned to ripping copy on the large newsroom desk.

"But Mickey," I pleaded, "you know I hate animals."

"You'll have fun," he said without looking up from his work. "It's just a promotion thing. There will be elephant keepers walking alongside controlling the animal and you just have to sit up there and go around in a circle."

So, with a great deal of reluctance, I found myself on a balmy spring day at the Cleveland Zoo. But instead of the enclosed elephant pavilion, I found myself on the large field in the center of the zoo. The zoo staff had decided not to let us ride their elephants; rather, they had brought in some privately-owned elephants.

My colleagues, "Big Chuck" Schodowski and Bob "Houlihan" Wells were already mounted on two of the smaller elephants when I arrived. A huge elephant with the unlikely name of Pansy was waiting for me.

A rather grubby elephant handler, with one leg shorter than the other, prompted some immediate speculation in my mind as to just how his leg had gotten shorter. Perhaps the elephant had eaten it!

The handler barked "DOWN!" and I was already lying on the ground when I realized he was talking to the elephant, who was ponderously squatting down on the ground.

"Just step on her leg, grab her ear, and pull yourself on top of her head," he ordered.

"Won't stepping on her leg make her upset or something?" I asked timidly.

"Nah," he grumbled at me. "She won't even feel it."

Stepping on her leg was like stepping on a rather soft rock. Pansy's ear felt like dusty leather as I tentatively grabbed and tried to jump onto her neck.

Pansy snorted softly a couple of times as I tried, time after time, to crawl, jump, or pull myself up her side and onto her neck. Finally the handler, still grumbling, walked over. As I was desperately pulling

Pansy's ear and had one leg nearly onto her neck, he placed a hand on my rear end and pushed with such force that I flew up onto the neck and right off the other side.

To the laughter of the assembled crowd, I picked myself up and sheepishly walked around the front of Pansy, who, at that moment, raised her trunk and snorted right in my face, giving me the full benefit of elephant morning breath—a cross between sewer gas and the scent of skunks.

With a reeling stomach, a red face, and grim determination, I again stepped onto Pansy's spongy knee and, this time, was able to clumsily spring onto the elephant's neck.

There was no saddle, just a sort of halter that the elephant wore over her head. A large leather strap was the only thing to hang onto.

"Grip your legs just behind her ears and hang on tight to that halter," the grumbling attendant offered.

I was just trying to figure out how to pinch my legs around something that large when the attendant barked, "UP, PANSY. UP!" The elephant lurched to her feet, nearly putting me on the ground again as I grabbed the leather strap and hung on for dear life, a scream of terror bubbling up in my throat.

I suddenly found myself towering 12 feet above the ground, looking down on the hundreds of people who had gathered to watch the spectacle. It was also at this point I realized that straddling the neckbone of this elephant was like straddling a rip-saw blade.

Swaying on top of the beast, I watched as the limping keeper herded Pansy into a line with the two elephants that Big Chuck and Houlihan were atop.

We posed for pictures. I wore a nervous smile, trying to both watch the cameras and keep an eye on Pansy's handler down below to make sure he didn't decide to go off and leave me alone on top of the elephant.

Chuck Voracec, the Zoo's public relations director, told the crowd that they were about to witness the first-ever elephant race at the Cleveland Zoo. I was looking around to see what elephants were going to race when, with a feeling of stark terror, I realized he was talking about the elephant I was astride, and the other two. Before I could utter even a gurgle of protest, someone raised a starter's pistol and fired a blast into the air and we were off.

We lumbered at a fast walk across the field. My limping handler seemed to be keeping up with some difficulty. I turned to see where the other two elephants were and realized that I was quite far out in front. I turned to call down to the handler to suggest we might slow down, and to my shock I found no one there.

I swiveled the other way, bringing a sharp stab of pain to the area between my legs, and to my dismay saw Pansy's handler limping and running and swearing as the elephant steadily left him in the dust. I was on board a runaway elephant!

In the next few moments many thoughts raced through my mind, most of them concerning death and dismemberment. I wondered, how do you stop a runaway elephant? I tried "Whoaa!" Pansy was oblivious. I pleaded with her, "Stop! Please Stop!" No good. Pansy lumbered on, heading toward the flamingo pens on the other side of the field, her speed increasing. With each stride I would fly up several inches and then slam back down on her razor sharp back. Each time that I flew into the air I could see her massive feet below and my imagination went wild with thoughts of how I would look if I flew off and ended up squished between her toes.

Over my shoulder, Pansy's keeper and the other elephants were getting farther and farther away. I debated trying to jump from the top of the elephant, but then I would run the risk of being trampled by her back feet. Just as I was about to give up hope, Pansy suddenly stopped. I almost tumbled headfirst to the ground as her head went down and she started grazing on some flowers that were planted along the edge of the walk.

This gave her swearing, limping keeper a chance to catch up. Relief washed over me. I was almost giddy with the thought of getting off that elephant's back. The keeper placed his elephant hook in her harness and gave a command.

"UP PANSY!" he shouted.

I was expecting the animal to kneel so I could get off, not raise up on her hind feet. I suddenly found myself hanging by both hands from her harness fifteen to twenty feet in the air as the keeper yelled to me, "SMILE AND WAVE AT THE CROWD!"

I was incredulous! Here I was hanging straight down the elephant's back, clinging to the harness with such ferocity that it would have taken three men to get my hands loose, and he wanted me to wave to the crowd! In fact, when Pansy finally did kneel and they told me I could get off, he did have to pry my fingers from the harness. It took three weeks for the bruises on my inner thighs to fade.

To this day, when I walk by the elephant exhibit at the zoo I get a little nervous. I have never had the slightest desire to ride another elephant.

CLEVELAND METROPARKS ZOO AND RAINFOREST

To my knowledge they don't have elephant races anymore, but they do have a new, state-of-the-art rainforest that has attracted a lot of attention nationwide. The zoo is one of the finest in the state and offers a lot of things to do with the family.

Cleveland Metroparks Zoo and Rainforest   (216) 661-7511
3900 Brookside Drive
Cleveland, Ohio   Handicapped access: yes

THE COLUMBUS ZOO

The Columbus Zoo became nationally known under its former director, Jack Hanna, a frequent guest on television's "Tonight Show." Even though Hanna has moved on to greener pastures, the zoo is still ranked as one of the top in the country. It is a major breeding center for lowland gorillas, cheetahs, and polar bears—all contained in a 404-acre park where the animals are kept in environmental compounds that closely resemble their natural habitats.

The Columbus Zoo   614-889-9471
9990 Riverside Drive
Powell, Ohio 43065 (Powell is a suburb on Columbus' NORTHWEST side.)
Handicapped access: yes

A ZOO AND HOLIDAY LIGHT FESTIVAL

The Cincinnati Zoo is considered one of the nation's top five zoos. It has one of the largest collections of rare animals in America, including 21 types of rare and endangered wild cats. They have "Colossus," the largest lowland gorilla in captivity, and they also offer a "Jungle Trails" exhibit, which is a naturalized rainforest where exotic animals from Asia and Africa live.

At Christmastime, the zoo is converted into one of the best holiday light festivals in Ohio. It's a time of year when you have two reasons to visit the zoo.

Cincinnati Zoo and Botanical Gardens　　　(513) 559-7724
3400 Vine Street　　　　　　　　　　　　FAX: (513) 559-779
Cincinnati, Ohio 45220　　　　　　　Handicapped access: yes

THE AKRON ZOO

While not as big as some of the other zoos in the state, Akron's well-kept facility offers a close-up look at animals from all over the world. Here, too, they turn the zoo into a holiday light festival in November and December.

Akron Zoo　　　　　　　　　　(216) 375-2525
500 Edgewood Drive
Akron, Ohio 44307　　　　　　Handicapped access: yes

THE TOLEDO ZOO

Small but highly regarded, Toledo's zoo offers both year-round exhibits of animals from all over the world and a light festival at Christmastime. Many of the animal enclosures have been built to look as if the animals were in their native wild habitats.

Toledo Zoo　　　　　　　　　　(419) 385-5751
2700 Broadway
Toledo, Ohio 43609　　　　　　Handicapped access: yes

3 **Just For Kids**

SOMETHING RELATIVELY NEW on the museum scene is the museum just for children—where there are no "Do Not Touch" signs, no "Keep Off" warnings, or pleas to be quiet. Instead, at these museums children are encouraged to touch, feel, pull, push, and otherwise use the exhibits. Imaginations can run wild. Noisy, squeaky, squealy kinds of things add to the cacophony of hundreds of excited kids, who are not only having fun but learning valuable lessons from the many creative displays.

Living in Ohio, we are close to many top children's museums; each makes a great destination for a One Tank Trip.

A PLACE OF BRIDGES

The Cleveland Children's Museum has a wonderful exhibit that celebrates the many bridges to be found in Cleveland. Kids can go in, around, and over the display. Not only is this exhibit fun, it also teaches youngsters the importance of bridges to a city's economy.

While this museum is much smaller than many similar museums, it offers a wide range of changing exhibits, as well as storytelling, toymaking, and a host of other activities to keep children entertained.

Cleveland Children's Museum   216-791-KIDS or 791-7114
10730 Euclid Avenue
Cleveland, Ohio 44106   Handicapped access: yes

CINCINNATI CHILDREN'S MUSEUM

This children's museum opened in 1994 in a former railroad warehouse along the Ohio River. It already has more than 35,000 square feet of displays on three floors, and has options on two more floors in the giant building.

On the first floor, there are displays that will entertain and educate preschoolers—everything from a fishing exhibit with real water, where kids fish with magnets to reel in metal fish, to a place where they can roll balls down a hill and see the difference in speed when the hill is straight or curved. On the second floor, older youngsters can take part in television special effects, learn about assembly lines, try their hands at making things, and turn giant gears by walking on a treadmill. On the third floor, there are oversized musical instruments (made by the same designer who created the floor piano that Tom Hanks danced on in the movie "Big") and much more. I even caught several adults trying out some of the exhibits and enjoying them as much as the kids.

The Cincinnati Children's Museum
Longworth Hall
Pete Rose Way
Cincinnati, Ohio   Handicapped access: yes

A CANADIAN FUNHOUSE

Across Lake Erie in London, Ontario is one of the finest children's museums I have seen, located in an old elementary school. One exhibit features an igloo, where youngsters can try on a parka, climb astride a snowmobile, and put on real snow shoes. Another is dedicated to professions. Here, youngsters can dress up in real uniforms of firefighters, doctors, utility workers or sewer workers. In fact, a mock sewer runs beneath the floor for children to explore.

In another wing of the building, children can dig in a sandpit for prehistoric fossils or dress up in dinosaur costumes. On another floor, a child-sized physics laboratory offers fun experiments for big and little kids.

London Regional Children's Museum   519-434-5726
21 Wharncliffe Road South
London, Ontario, Canada N6J 4G5   Handicapped access: yes

FLY AN AIRPLANE OR SIT ON A FROG

In Flint, Michigan, there is a small but exciting children's museum that offers a real airplane for kids to climb in and on. There is also a five-foot-tall stone frog. Add to these several work-related exhibits—such as a courtroom and jail, television studio, and grocery store—where kids can play the role of adult, and you have a fun place for youngsters and parents.

Flint Children's Museum   313-238-6900
432 North Saginaw St.
Flint, Michigan 48503   Handicapped access: yes

THE BIGGEST IN THE MIDWEST

Indianapolis, Indiana boasts the largest children's museum in the midwest. The museum has received wide attention for its many exciting exhibits, including a full-size, working, antique carousel that kids can ride. Some exhibits specifically address the needs of teenagers and include sophisticated fun with science, ecology, and mathematics. This is truly a museum with something for every age group.

Indianapolis Children's Museum   317-924-5431
3000 North Meridian St.
Indianapolis, Indiana   Handicapped access: yes

One Tank Tip #2
Save With Discounts

When booking a motel be sure to ask for any discounts they may offer such as special corporate rates or senior citizen prices. You may be pleasantly surprised by the amount of the savings.

4 Regional Foods I Have Known and Sometimes Loved

IN CINCINNATI—BESIDES THE CHILI—it's goetta and eggs. In Wilmot, it's an Amish wedding spread. In Chardon, it's pancakes and sauerkraut.

In many towns and regions of Ohio there is a favorite food that, though popular with the locals, just doesn't seem to catch on with the rest of us. In some cases, that's probably because we never heard of it. In other cases, it may just be that the environment gives area residents some different tastebuds.

GOETTA

Just what the heck is goetta, and why do Cincinnatians think it's so great? While Cincinnati chili may be better known, a true sign that you are dealing with a Cincinnati native is when they sit down to breakfast and order goetta with their eggs. This combination of cornmeal and ground sausage, ham, bacon, or all of the above is blended with seasonings, stuffed into a sausage casing, then sliced and fried. You can find goetta at just about any Cincinnati restaurant that serves breakfast. For help in finding a place, contact these folks for a few suggestions:

> **Greater Cincinnati Convention and Visitors Bureau** 800-543-2613
> 200 West Sixth Street
> Cincinnati, Ohio 45202-2361

BELLYSTICKERS

In the tiny northwest Ohio town of Archbold they make a concoction known as bellystickers. These are not for the diet-conscious. They're sort of like sinful Parker House rolls. In fact, they start out as fresh-baked Parker House rolls, then fresh cream and sugar are poured on top and allowed to seep through overnight. The next morning, the pan is inverted on a plate and the bellystickers are served. If you don't care about calories, it's a wonderful way to start the day.

The Barn Restaurant and Dough Box Bakery   419-446-2541
State Route 2
Archbold, Ohio 43502   Handicapped access: yes

AN AMISH WEDDING SPREAD

The Amish areas of Ohio feature a wonderful snack concoction known as an "Amish Wedding Spread." There are several different recipes. The one I like best is a combination of peanut butter, marshmallow, and maple syrup blended and served on fresh homemade Amish bread. It is difficult to write about without salivating.

The Amish Door Restaurant   216-359-5464
U.S. Route 6
Wilmot, Ohio 44689

PANCAKES, SYRUP, AND . . . SAUERKRAUT

In the northeast Ohio town of Chardon, during the annual Maple Festival you can find pancakes served with fresh-made maple syrup and . . . sauerkraut! I know, I can hear you saying, "YUKK!" already. That was my reaction, too, before I tried it. But the taste—sweet and sour and reminiscent of a Chinese egg roll, was very good. The Maple festival is held each year on the first weekend after Easter. We had our pancakes and sauerkraut at:

The Masonic Temple   216-286-3007
Chardon, Ohio 44024
For more information about the festival, call:

MORE SYRUP

Maple syrup can be found in many areas of Ohio. Several places offer demonstrations of "sugaring," the boiling of maple sap into syrup and candy. We have found some great bargains in fresh maple syrup in Geauga County by following handmade signs to Amish homes where you can buy direct from the farmers who make it.

BRATS

They call them brats in Bucyrus. Bratwurst sausage is a German invention that has become a staple in this central Ohio town. In fact, a festival honoring the sausage is held here each year. Bratwurst is fresh pork and spices ground up and packed into links that are then grilled over charcoal fires until they split open. Slathered with mustard, sauerkraut, or horseradish sauce, they can almost be a meal by themselves. One brat-maker here even has a drive-through restaurant.

W.P.I. Drive Thru Bakery and Restaurant   419-562-3332
700 North Sandusky Street
Bucyrus, Ohio 44820   Handicapped access: yes

KETTLE CHIPS

In Elyria, there is a small company that makes potato chips the way they ought to be made; they leave in the chips that get slightly burned. Thomasson's Potato Chips also lets you buy right at the factory. If you stop out on weekday mornings, when they are cooking, you can buy what they call a "hot kettle bag." They take a large bag, hold it at the end of the conveyor line as the fresh chips come out of the cooker, and fill it to overflowing. One of the most delicious bargains in town.

Thomasson's Potato Chips   216-322-0223
156 Cook Court
Elyria, Ohio 44035   Handicapped access: yes

SPECIAL RECIPE LEMONADE

Lemonade is the drink of choice for many in Bellevue, Ohio. McClain's Restaurant and Old Tyme Saloon has been a fixture downtown for more than a century. The craze for lemonade started during prohibition when the present owner's grandfather would mix up a batch of "special recipe" lemonade for thirsty regular customers. The lemonade was, allegedly, liberally laced with illegal hooch. When prohibition ended and McClain's could legally sell booze again, customers still demanded the special recipe lemonade. Today, McClain's is a tavern and family restaurant known for good ribs as well as lemonade—both kinds.

McClain's Restaurant and Old Tyme Saloon   419-483-2727
137 East Main St.
Bellevue, Ohio 44811

5 The Day The Circus Came To Town

"DO A FEATURE ON THE CIRCUS that's in town," assignment editor Mickey Flanagan said.

"Like what?" I came back.

"Oh, you'll find something to do," he said. "You know, like try out for the trapeze act, or something."

"I think I'll do the 'or something,'" I replied as I went out the door.

The Circus Vargas was one of the last circuses still working under canvas and doing one-night stands across the Midwest. It was set up for a weekend run in a Willowick shopping center parking lot. The only problem was that the trucks carrying the tents and some of the rigging had broken down, and it was only a couple of hours to show-time. It looked like this circus was instead going to be a performance under the stars, because in the best tradition of show business, the "show must go on."

The circus public relations man was understandably a bit harried, considering that his circus was about to put on a performance in the middle of a parking lot without tents.

"The only act that can talk to you right now is Vashock!" he announced as he led me through ropes and cables and around a lion's cage.

Vashock turned out to be a small blond man with a thick Czechoslovakian accent who, I learned, did a high-wire act with his wife on a motorcycle. The motorcycle, which had no tires on it, was driven on its rims up a steel cable to a spot about forty feet over the lion's cage, at what would have been the top of the tent.

I was asking him just what the rest of the act consisted of when he interrupted to tell me that we were using up his rehearsal time and he wanted to make a couple of practice runs up the cable. "Vy dahnt you come along," he said.

I gulped and looked at the steep cable that ran to the top of a huge pole over the cage where the lions and tigers were now pacing. Videographer Gary Korb urged me on.

"Go ahead!" Korb said. "You know they want some reporter involvement in these stories."

"I don't think that looks too safe," I replied, again tilting my head back to see how far up the cable ran.

"You don't think he'd let you do anything dangerous," Gary said. "He'll probably just take you up a few feet and then come right back down."

Vashock stood there smiling, saying, "Yah, Yah. Ve gif you short ride."

The motorcycle was already sitting on the wire, atop a wooden stand, about six feet off the ground. Beneath it, attached to the motorcycle, was a steel trapeze with straps on each side. I sat down on the trapeze and Vashock immediately began strapping my hands to the side bars.

"Why are you doing this ?" I asked, nervously.

"Because I dahn't want you to be scared and jump off," he replied as he climbed onto the motorcycle above me and kick-started it. Whatever I said in reply was lost in the roar of the motorcycle. We started to move. I grabbed the steel bars with an iron grip as we went up, and up, and up. I finally opened my eyes and looked down. Below me, looking directly up at me was the largest lion I have ever seen in my life and his mouth was open, teeth gleaming!

Just then the motorcycle shut off and we sat there gently swaying back and forth, balanced on a single, silvery steel cable 40 feet over the lions and the blacktop parking lot.

"How you lak this?" Vashock shouted down to me.

I was too frightened to answer. I managed to look at him and open my mouth, but not a word would come out. Finally I was able to work my lips into a slight grimace, which Vashock immediately mistook for a smile of encouragement.

"Maybe we do a couple of loop-loops!" he shouted down to me as he started to swing the motorcycle in a crazy side-to-side motion. My weight was the only thing that was keeping the cycle on the wire!

"D-D-D-DOWN!" I finally managed to get out.

"Down?" Vashock said perplexed.

"Yes, take me DOWN!" I shouted. "I forgot something on the ground."

"Okeydokey," Vashock answered as he fired up the motorcycle and we started coasting backwards, back towards the ground.

When we were finally back down and my hands had been pried from the trapeze bar, Vashock asked me,

"Vot did you forget?"

"My courage," I truthfully replied. "Why did you take me all the way to the top?"

He smiled, a bit sheepishly.

"Mine rigging is still on the truck that is not here," he explained, "and I had to use someone else's cables and mine wife is pregnant and I didn't want her on board when I tested the cables. I think, if it don't break with you on board trapeze, it is safe for her to do the show."

The traveling circus may almost be just a memory, but there are lots of family fun places still left here in northern Ohio—particularly amusement parks, from century-old Geauga Lake, with its modern-day theme park attractions, to a place that has remained unchanged for generations: Memphis Kiddie Park.

MEMPHIS KIDDIE PARK

If you were a youngster growing up in the 1950s on the west side of Cleveland, chances are you probably spent some of your summer days at Memphis Kiddie Park in Brooklyn. The good news is that absolutely nothing has changed there in over 40 years. The very same rides, the tiny merry-go-round, the mini–roller-coaster, the little Ferris wheel, and the kiddie train that passes Snow White and the seven concrete dwarfs are all just as they were back in 1950, though perhaps a different color. Bill Applegarth, who was running it back in the 1950s, is still in charge, keeping all the rides running and creating memories for his latest generation of customers.

Memphis Kiddie Park   216-941-5995
10340 Memphis Avenue
Brooklyn, Ohio 44144   Handicapped access: yes

GEAUGA LAKE AMUSEMENT PARK

Now in its second century of entertaining northern Ohio, this park is nationally known for its wooden roller coaster, which is a favorite with coaster enthusiasts. From a wave-action pool to live entertainment, this is a fun destination for everyone in the family.

Geauga Lake Amusement Park 216-562-7131
1060 Aurora Road
Aurora, Ohio 44202   Handicapped access: yes

SEA WORLD OF OHIO

This is the home of Shamu the whale and all his friends, including dolphins, penguins, and exotic birds. The park is seasonal and attracts huge crowds in the summertime. It also offers several wintertime educational programs to schools and other organizations.

Sea World of Ohio   216-562-8101
1100 Sea World Drive
Aurora, Ohio 44202   Handicapped access: yes

AMUSEMENT PARK BOOKS

While Euclid Beach Park now remains only in spirit—in the nostalgic thoughts of the folks who grew up spending summers riding the rides and enjoying the lakefront views, a publishing company has printed a pictorial history of Euclid Beach Park (and one on Conneaut Lake, too). They are books full of memories.

Amusement Park Books
20925 Mastick Road
Fairview Park, Ohio 44126

EUCLID BEACH, THE CATALOGUE

Though Euclid Beach Park may be gone, the family that once operated it is still in business—producing memories of the park. The Humphrey Company still makes the famous popcorn balls and taffy that were Euclid Beach trademarks. They sell gift boxes by mail and in area gift stores. For a catalog, write to:

The Humphrey Company   216-481-7575
11 Magnolia Drive
Cleveland, Ohio 44110   No store, mail order only

6 Hamburgers and Ice-Cream Cones

WE ALL KNOW THAT there is no ham in hamburger, but there almost was. Two brothers, Charles and Frank Menches, from Canton, were running a food tent at the Erie County Fair in Hamburg, New York in 1885. Their specialties were a freshly ground sausage sandwich, orange cider, oysters, and cigars. They would use fresh pork, add their own ingredients and spices to it, and then press it into a patty shape and fry it on a grill for hungry fair-goers.

The sausage sandwiches sold well, but fate intervened. That summer was so hot that butchers did not dare slaughter any pigs, so there was a sausage shortage. Frank went searching local suppliers and could only come up with ground beef. They decided to try it, but it didn't taste quite right, so they tried other seasonings—coffee, brown sugar, and other things. They liked the taste. More importantly, their customers loved it, and when one asked what they called the sandwich, Frank Menches, looking at the name of the town, "Hamburg", on a nearby banner, replied,

"It's a Hamburger!"

And so was born the sandwich that would spawn a million imitations and become the symbol of American food.

But history was not done with the Menches brothers. At the 1904 St. Louis World's Fair, they were peddling their "hamburgers" and selling homemade ice cream served on some fresh waffles. Reportedly, a young girl who didn't want to sit down to eat her ice cream asked for some way to take it with her. One of the Menches brothers had an inspiration: he grabbed a fresh waffle from the waffle-maker, took one of this tent pegs, wrapped the waffle around it to make a cone, and then placed the ice cream inside it.

The ice cream cone was born.

Today, the Menches brothers' great-great-grandchildren have discovered the brothers' original hamburger recipe and have opened a restaurant in Green, Ohio where they serve both the original-recipe hamburgers, made with coffee, brown sugar, and a "secret ingredient," and homemade waffle ice cream cones.

Menches Brothers Original Hamburgers   (216) 896-2288
3700 Massillon Road, Suite 130
Uniontown, Ohio 44685   Handicapped access: yes

A PARK FOR ALL PEOPLE

The Stark County Park District has attempted to make Sippo Lake a park that everyone—old, young, middle-aged, and the physically challenged—can enjoy. For openers, there is the fishing pier, the largest inland fishing pier in Ohio. The picnic area is built in the shape of a pirate ship on the tree-shaded shore of the lake.

You can rent a rowboat for a dollar an hour, and small motor boats are equally inexpensive. In the marina you'll find one of the largest fishing tackle collections in the state.

For the youngsters there is a nature center, where abandoned and injured wildlife is cared for and nursed back to health, as well as an outstanding display of stuffed animals from around the world.

Perception Park, just across the lake, is dedicated to physically challenged people. There is an all-people's paved path that leads to the lake, with sturdy park benches along the edge of the path. All picnic tables are wheelchair accessible, as are the barbecue grills. There is a ramp that leads to a gazebo at the edge of the lake. All restrooms are also accessible to the handicapped. Best of all, admission to the park is free.

Sippo Lake Park   (216) 477-3552
Stark County Park District, 5300 Tyner Avenue, N.W.
Canton, Ohio 44708   Handicapped access: yes

A FLOATING CHAPEL

Portage Lakes offers one of the more unusual places to embark on the seas of matrimony. Here, you can be married on board a floating chapel.

This was the idea of two clergy, who happen to be man and wife; they have turned their large float boat into a seagoing wedding chapel. The boat comes complete with wedding decorations, wedding music, and two ministers to officiate. All you have to do is provide the bride and groom and a marriage license.

Chapel on the Lake   (216) 673-1567
657 Longmere Dr.
Kent, Ohio 44240   Handicapped access: yes

7 **Read the Fine Print**

"REMEMBER, YOU HAVE a speech tomorrow in Warren, Ohio," my wife Bonnie reminded me.

"On a Monday morning?" I asked.

"Check the calendar," she replied as she walked out of the room.

I walked to the desk and there it was circled on my calendar: March 19th, 1992, Packard Music Hall, Warren, Ohio, 9:00 a.m. Speech.

The alarm clock rang at six o'clock on Monday morning. Outside, a late winter snow was falling and early radio newscasters were warning motorists to prepare for a long drive to work.

I drove across the Ohio Turnpike wondering if the weather would affect the turnout at the speech I was to make. Spun-out trucks dotted the turnpike median strip and it was a white-knuckle trip every mile of the way.

At 8:45 a.m. I reached the Packard Music Hall parking lot. It was empty. My tire tracks in the fresh snow were the only ones there. I drove to the rear of the building. No cars there. Perhaps I was early. I waited.

Fifteen minutes later, when the speech was to have started, I was still the only one in the parking lot. I picked up my cellular phone and called Kevin Salyer at TV8, who had set up the speech.

"Kevin", I said, with some sarcasm, "I just drove through a snowstorm to Warren, Ohio, and no one is here."

"Let me check the invitation," he replied. "I'll be right back."

There was a short pause and then he came back on the phone.

"Do you have the copy of the invitation I gave you?" he asked, an sarcastic tinge in his voice.

"Certainly!" I replied, "It's right here on the seat beside me."

"Read the date to me," he said.

"Just like I told you", I began, "March 19th, 9:00 a.m."

"No", he said, "the WHOLE date."

I looked at the letter again and read, "March 19th, 1993." I had arrived at the speech too early. One year too early.

A WARREN TRADITION

Just about anyone who has ever lived in Warren, or even just stopped by for a visit, has had at least one hotdog at this downtown

Warren institution. Here they have a secret, closely guarded sauce that they use on the hotdogs, and they go through hundreds of hotdogs every day. Many fans buy the dogs by the bagful.

The Hot Dog Shoppe   (216) 395-7057
740 West Market Street
Warren, Ohio 44481   Handicapped access: step into restaurant

WHERE CELEBRITIES STAY AND PLAY

In Warren, it's the Avalon Inn that attracts both local folks and the rich and famous who visit here. A fine restaurant, lovely rooms, and a championship golf course with beautiful grounds make this a great getaway for families. Some of the biggest names in golf have played this course.

The Avalon Inn   (216)-856-1900
9519 East Market Street
Warren, Ohio 44484   Handicapped access: yes

THE GHOSTS OF THE PAST

Warren offers a unique Halloween tradition. Each October, the Fine Arts Council gets actors to portray famous residents who once lived along "Millionaires' Row." In the evening, as you walk along the street, "ghosts" of these residents drift out to the street to tell stories of grief and scandal that they faced. The tour ends at a pioneer cemetery, where a tombstone that marks the graves of two little boys is pointed out. One boy died several years earlier than the other. The family had a second son and gave him the first son's name. The second son died on the very same day and month as his brother and at the same young age!

Of course celebrating Halloween is not the only thing the Fine Arts Council does for the city. Write or call them for a current schedule of events.

Fine Arts Council of Trumbull County   (216) 399-1212
303 Mahoning Avenue, N.W.
Warren, Ohio 44483   Handicapped access: yes

FOR REALLY BIG APPETITES

How about "mile-high" pie or a "plowboy" sandwich? These are just two of the staples on the menu at this family-style restaurant in

Trumbull County. The pie has so much filling and meringue that it looks more like a basketball! The sandwich features a veal cutlet that fills an entire steak platter and dwarfs the huge Kaiser roll on which it is served. All the food here is made from scratch each day. This is definitely a place where the local folks eat.

Burghill Country Inn Restaurant   (216) 772-7741
5346 Youngstown-Conneaut Road (State Route 7)
Burghill, Ohio 44404   Handicapped access: yes

SEARCHING FOR FLEAS

If you're looking for antiques, or just someone else's old junk, you can probably find it here. This building, which formerly held tennis courts, has been reborn as an antique mall and flea market. Dozens of dealers are on hand to help you find just about anything you are looking for.

Hubbard-Liberty Flea Market and Antique Mall 216-534-9855
5959 West Liberty (Route 304)
Hubbard, Ohio 44425   Handicapped access: yes

A SWEET TOUR

If you are a confirmed chocoholic, don't miss this stop. At this candy company, you can walk above the factory and watch—and smell—all that delicious chocolate being cooked and poured into molds to make your favorite treat. There is also a gift shop here where you can buy freshly made chocolates. Look for their broken candies, which they sell as seconds at reduced prices.

Costello's Candy Factory   (216) 545-0325
39 West Liberty
Girard, Ohio 44420   Handicapped access: yes

MORE INFORMATION

Check for maps, brochures, and other ideas, if you're planning a visit to Trumbull County by calling or writing:

Trumbull County Convention and Visitor's Bureau (216) 544-3468
650 Youngstown-Warren Road
Niles, Ohio 44446   Handicapped access: yes

8 A School's Home is Its Castle

STRANGERS WANDERING INTO the Alliance City School District's office often do a double take. The main hall is guarded by a life-size suit of armor. In the rotunda is a crystal chandelier, a duplicate of one presented years ago to the Shah of Iran. There are secret passages, a swimming pool, and a bowling alley, as well as a wine cellar and a ballroom.

Welcome to Glamorgan Castle, and yes, it really is the office of the Alliance City Schools.

The Castle was built in 1904 as a private residence for Alliance industrialist Colonel William Henry Morgan. It cost $400,000 and took five years to build. The stone walls above the ground are a minimum of 13 inches thick.

The property had many owners down through the years. It served as the home of the local Elks Lodge, and then as corporate headquarters for the Alliance Machine Company. In 1973, through a series of federal grants, the Castle and 20 acres of land were turned over to the Alliance Schools.

Tours can be arranged by calling the school district office during the school year. Group tours can sometimes be arranged for other times.

Glamorgan Castle   (216) 821-2100
200 Glamorgan Street
Alliance, Ohio 44601   Handicapped access: steps in building

Glamorgan Castle

GRINDERS FOR LUNCH

In case you are wondering what the heck a grinder is, it's like a "submarine" sandwich. Lots of meat, cheese, and veggies served on a chewy roll. But here they serve much more—everything from Cajun Steak to Santa Fe Chicken. And then there are the desserts. Specialties are the banana split pie and the "choc-o-holic" brownie sundae. This is where you'll find a lot of local folks at lunchtime and dinnertime.

Grinders and Such   (216) 821-6665
1820 West State Street
Alliance, Ohio 44601   Handicapped access: yes

LIBRARY IN A MALL

If you have family members who hate to shop, take them along to the Carnation Mall in Alliance, where you'll find one of the only public libraries located in a shopping mall. They can browse, relax in the reading room, or check out books while the rest of the family goes shopping.

Rodman Public Library   PH: (216) 821-1313
Carnation Mall, 2500 West State Street
Alliance, Ohio 44601   Handicapped access: yes
Open 9–9 Mon–Thu; 9–5:30 Fri & Sat

SLEEP AND SHOP

You can spend the night in a shopping mall here in Alliance, Ohio. The Comfort Inn anchors one end of the Carnation Shopping Mall. The hotel offers many amenities: whirlpool baths in some rooms, an indoor swimming pool, an exercise room, and packages that include tickets to the movie theaters just off the lobby or dinner in your room served by a restaurant in the mall.

Comfort Inn   (216) 821-5555 or (800) 948-5555
Carnation Mall, 2500 West State Street
Alliance, Ohio 44601   Handicapped access: yes

A BASKET FACTORY

This is one of the newest tourist attractions in Alliance. Some of the basketmakers here used to work for the Longaberger Basket

Company. You can tour the plant and watch them weave oak and maple strips into ornate baskets both for decoration and for utilitarian purposes, like market baskets, firewood containers,and magazine holders. They also have a company store where you can buy both top quality baskets and some of their "seconds," baskets that have slight flaws. Each basket is signed and dated by the basketmaker. Many of these baskets have or will become collectibles.

Carnation Country Crafts   (216) 823-7231
170 East Market Street
Alliance, Ohio 44601   Handicapped access: steps to factory on second floor

WHERE THE BUFFALO ROAM

One of the larger privately owned buffalo, or bison, herds in Ohio is located not far from Alliance. The owner offers tours of the ranch where he raises the animals for meat and hides.

Winter seems to be a good time to visit and see the young calves cavorting in the fields. The meat of the bison is becoming popular with folks who are watching their fat intake. Nutritionists say that bison meat is less fatty than beef or even turkey.

1880 Buffalo Ranch   (216) 877-6494
2545 Pontius Street, N.E.
Hartville, Ohio 44632   Tours by reservation
Handicapped access: gravel and dirt paths to barn and fields.

A COAT FACTORY TOUR

The Sherwood Coat Factory, which makes women's coats, calls downtown Alliance home. In fact, their factory is in an old O'Neil department store. You can take a tour of the plant, watch coats being made, and then visit the company's factory outlet store, where overruns, discontinued styles, and seconds are sold—sometimes at a savings of as much as 90 percent. The store is open Monday through Saturday. Factory tours are only available during working hours, and it is best to call for reservations. You can also buy some of their surplus material and sewing thread in the store.

Sherwood Factory Outlet   (216) 823-4020
45 Arch Street
Alliance, Ohio 44601   Handicapped access: yes

A HEALTHY PLACE TO EAT

While the owners here didn't set out to specialize in health-conscious meals, they decided not to deep-fry foods but broil them instead because that tastes better. The result has been good food that is also healthy, and this small restaurant attracts a lot of people for its medium-priced meals. The restaurant is open seven days a week.

Taster's Choice Cafe   (216) 821-6666
1908 South Union Avenue
Alliance, Ohio 44601   Handicapped access: yes

AN OLD FASHIONED BANANA SPLIT

This candy store, soda fountain, and sandwich shop has been a Stark County institution for generations. Heggy's Candies are famous in many parts of the state, but local folks also head for Heggy's for fountain treats like old-fashioned banana splits made with vanilla, chocolate, and strawberry ice cream and mounded with whipped cream and cherries. It's the kind of place where you think about putting off that diet you were going to start today until tomorrow.

Heggy's Candies   (216) 821-2051
1306 West State Street
Alliance, Ohio 44601   Handicapped access: yes

One Tank Tip #3
Ask About a Better Room

When registering at a motel be sure to inquire about upgrades in the room you have booked. Some motels and hotels offer same price upgrades to better rooms if it looks like they will not be busy and the better rooms would be empty.

9 Ohio's Own Flying Saucer

HOW MANY STATES CAN CLAIM to have a flying saucer as a permanent resident? Many a motorist traveling along U.S. Route 20 in northeast Ohio has done the proverbial double take on entering the town of Ashtabula. For there it sits, right where routes 11, 46, and 20 all come together—about 60 feet in diameter and perhaps 30 feet high with a clear bubble cockpit on the top! It looks abandoned, as though some alien space pilot landed many years ago to sample the pleasures of downtown Ashtabula and never returned.

The real story is less romantic. The "saucer" was built back in the late 1950s as a gasoline station. Its futuristic design was intended to capitalize on the space and UFO craze that was then sweeping the country. The perimeter of the saucer was lined with blinking, pulsating lights to attract customers. At Christmastime, the owner used to prop a mannequin of Santa Claus in the clear bubble-like cockpit on top of the saucer.

Customers were heard to ask the attendant if Captain Kirk of the Starship Enterprise was aboard.

But with the arrival of interstate highways and shopping malls, traffic patterns changed and eventually the flying saucer gasoline station closed its doors and removed the gasoline pumps.

There has been talk over the last few years of new businesses or perhaps a tourist information center making use of the old saucer landmark, but so far nothing has happened and Ohio's only flying saucer still sits earthbound and abandoned at an intersection in Ashtabula.

COVERED BRIDGE CAPITAL

The people of this county not only preserve their old covered bridges, they appreciate them so much they are building new ones! These bridges are economical and scenic as well as a tourist attraction. A covered bridge festival is held each autumn to celebrate the 14 bridges that now exist in Ohio's largest county. And more bridges will be completed soon. Maps of the bridges are available year-round from the festival headquarters in Jefferson.

Covered Bridge Festival   (216) 576-3769
25 West Jefferson Street
Jefferson, Ohio 44047   Handicapped access: yes

RAILROAD RIDE

There is a working railroad here in the county seat of Ashtabula County. On weekends, it also hauls tourists in antique passenger cars over a short line that runs through forests and swamps and near the town.

A C & J Railroad Company   (216) 576-6346
160 East Walnut Street, P.O. Box 222
Jefferson, Ohio 44047

CUT YOUR OWN CHRISTMAS TREES

Ashtabula offers some of the larger Christmas tree plantations in the state. Two of them provide a unique way to get your annual treat: ride a horse-drawn wagon back into the fields, cut your own tree, throw it on the wagon, and haul it back to the office. It makes a great family holiday tradition. Usually open from late November/early December until Christmas.

Manners Pine Tree Lodge   (216) 294-2444
780 Dodgeville Road
New Lyme, Ohio 44066   Handicapped access: steps to wagon

Henson's Hideaway Tree Farm and Nursery
1155 Brockway Road   (216) 294-2292
Rome, Ohio 44085   Handicapped access: yes

GO PROSPECTING

You can actually pan for diamonds and other precious stones here in Ashtabula County. The NOEMA Gem Mine is a unique business that lets you take a bucket and sift through "tailings" that they have purchased from mines around the world. Any precious or semi-precious stones are yours to keep. A jewelry business on site can mount any stone you find. While you may not find the Hope Diamond, they claim that most people do find some kind of semi-precious stone that can be turned into a necklace or bracelet.

NOEMA Gemstone Mine   (216) 275-3211
1788 Mill St.
Austinburg, Ohio 44010   Handicapped access: gravel driveway

A BABY-BUGGY MUSEUM

It's perhaps the only museum of its kind in the world. The Perambulator Museum started out as a hobby for two sisters and has now grown into a tourist attraction. Included in the collection is the Victorian perambulator used in the movie, Gone With The Wind. They also have early sleds and other conveyances used to transport children in the last two or three centuries. Many of the pieces on display are one-of-a-kind.

The Victorian Perambulator Museum of Jefferson   (216) 576-9588
26 East Cedar Street, off Route 46
Jefferson, Ohio 44047   Handicapped access: steps into house, narrow doorways

A TRUE HIDEAWAY

If you want to be truly alone, this is for you. A small cottage all by itself in the middle of a 400-acre farm, with its own 25-acre lake, stocked with fish. The cottage, which has several bedrooms, has electricity and running water but is rather rustic. There are pots and pans, but you must bring your own bedding and food. The cottage is rented by the week and sometimes, in the off-season, by the weekend.

Caroma Ranch Hideaway   (216) 583-2470
9499 State Route 46
North Bloomfield, Ohio 44450
Handicapped access: gravel roads to cottage, grass to edge of lake

ANIMATED CHRISTMAS DECORATIONS

This year-round Christmas store puts up a huge display of animated holiday scenes each year from October until New Year's Eve. There is everything from Santa and his elves in their North Pole workshop to a life-sized nativity scene. Admission is free but donations are accepted. The money is turned over to needy Ashtabula County families to help make their holidays brighter.

When the Christmas holiday is over, the exhibit is taken down and an Easter display of animated scenes takes its place.

Christmas World   (216) 997-9223
1760 West Prospect (Route 20)
Ashtabula, Ohio 44084   Handicapped access: yes

HISTORIC FRITTERS

Back in 1798, when this tavern was built, its cooks started making corn fritters for the dining room guests and now, nearly two hundred years later, they are still using the same recipe.

The famous landmark restaurant also serves many other tasty, made-from-scratch items that keep their customers coming back again and again.

The Olde Tavern at Unionville   (800) 7-TAVERN
7935 South Ridge Road (Route 84)
Unionville, Ohio   Handicapped access: yes

From My Mailbag...

Neil Zurcher:

My family and I took that trip you told about to Elmira, New York. We ran out of gas on the way there and had to call a tow truck to get going again. You ruined our afternoon. I am enclosing the bill for the tow truck and the gasoline to get back home. Please remit by return mail.

--Lost in New York

10 Wrong-Way River

"HOLD IT RIGHT THERE!" videographer Bill West shouted to me.

I was holding "it"—a canoe—by paddling frantically against the current in the Black Fork River here in Loudonville.

"Okay!" West shouted. "Paddle by me again and this time, SMILE!"

I gritted my teeth and sloshed the cold springtime water with my paddle. The current was so strong that I really had little to do other than keep the boat upright and steer it near the center of the river. I glided by West's photography station on the bank and once again started paddling hard against the current to stop the boat.

"Take it back up river again!" West called.

Once more I pushed and pulled on the paddle battling the current as the canoe bucked and twisted in the current. Finally, I worked my way about 200 feet upstream where I cautiously turned the canoe and grabbed onto an overhead tree limb to keep from scooting downstream again.

"You know, that water is cold," I offered to West as he set up his camera in a different location.

"Just remember to smile as you go by me and we'll be done here," he prodded me.

On West's signal I started paddling downstream again, trying to look like I did this every day of the week and was an old hand at canoeing.

But just as I passed West's position I felt the canoe rock. I grabbed the sides and hung on for dear life.

West shouted at me, "Aww, you screwed it up again! Take it back upstream."

The boat seemed to settle down and I reached for the paddle that I had dropped in the middle of the canoe. Then it happened.

My weight caused the boat to rock to the right, nearly overturning. I flung my weight to the opposite side, overreacting and overcorrecting, and the canoe started rocking the other way so violently that I knew I was going into the river.

I dropped the paddle and clawed at my hip pocket, flinging my wallet towards shore as I tried, at the same time, to tear off my non-waterproof watch and hurl it to shore. My arm was in midair when I went upside down into the cold river. Since the river is only about three feet deep in most areas, I hit bottom immediately and shot back to the surface.

"**&*%$#%^&," I shouted as I also spewed a mouthful of brown river water into the air. I regained my feet on the slippery river bottom and started to wade towards shore just in time to see my wallet starting to sink beneath the surface. There was no choice but to dive for it. I managed to retrieve it, and my hat, which had floated off my head in the capsizing.

Bill West stood on the bank, with a funny smile on his face and said, "I didn't have the camera running. If you did that intentionally we'll have to do it over."

Between curses, I informed him that it was NOT intentional and we would NOT do it again. Frankly, I was grateful that there was no footage of the embarrassing accident and that no one besides West had seen it.

While West went to shoot some more proficient canoers, I slopped my way back to the parking lot. It had turned into a sunny day, and I noticed that the parking lot was empty, save one woman at the other end. I tossed my wallet onto the trunk of our car. I spread out the sodden bills and cards. I peeled off my socks and shoes and laid them on the trunk to dry, and was just unbuttoning my shirt, when I noticed the woman was taking pictures of me.

Jo Lemon of the Ashland newspaper had heard we were in the area and had come to interview me. The following week, there I was in all my wet and bedraggled glory, on the front page of the newspaper, wringing out my socks. It gave her readers a first-hand look at the "glamour" of television.

A footnote: Dick Schrafrath, the former Cleveland Browns star, who operated the canoe livery where we were doing the taping, saw the segment and the next time I came asking for a canoe to use in a story, he offered me one with outrigger pontoons—sort of a canoe with training wheels!

Despite my problems, I found that the Loudonville area offers many fun things to do for the family.

Loudonville Canoe Livery   (419) 994-4161
424 West Main Street
Loudonville, Ohio 44842   Handicapped access: ramp to water

MOHICAN STATE PARK

This beautiful state park offers a lodge tucked away far from highways and towns. Hollywood types like Alan Alda and Paul Newman have stayed here more than once. Besides a modern lodge, cabins, camping, and seclusion, the park offers lakes with fishing, some great wooded hiking trails, and Ohio's Veterans' Memorial Chapel.

Mohican State Park   (419) 994-5125
P.O. Box 22
Loudonville, Ohio 44842   Handicapped access: yes

Mohican Park Lodge   (419) 938-5411
R.D. #2
Perrysville, Ohio 44864   Handicapped access: yes

Mohican State Park Lodge

OUTSIDE THE PARK

If you can't get into the lodge and want something better than a tent, try this motel chain near the interstate highway. It's a relatively new building that offers whirlpool baths in some suites, breakfast included, and a swimming pool—for a surprisingly low price.

Comfort Inn   (419) 886-4000
I-71 at State Route 97, 855 Comfort Plaza Drive
Bellville, Ohio 44813   Handicapped access: yes

THINGS TO DO

There are all the usual tourist things to do here. One of the long-time attractions is Mohican Family Fun Center. They have go-karts, horseback riding, and canoe and float trips. They are located just a short distance from Mohican State Park.

Mohican Family Fun Center   (800) MO-CANOE or (419) 994-3103 or 994-4020
Route 3 (1 mile south of Loudonville)
Loudonville, Ohio 44842   Handicapped access: yes to some attractions

---

One Tank Tip #4

Troop on in for a Map

If you need a map check state police posts along most major highways. They usually have state maps and usually they are free.

---

11 Ohio's Presidential Trail: William Mckinley

WILLIAM MCKINLEY WAS our 25th president. He was born in Niles, Ohio and spent most of his adult life in Canton. He was a major in the Civil War, served as a congressman from Ohio, and served three terms as governor of Ohio. Mckinley had been elected to his second term as president of the United States when he was assassinated, while speaking in Buffalo, New York in 1901. He was brought back to Canton and today his tomb dominates the city skyline. At the time of his death he became the third U.S. president in 36 years to be assassinated! The other two were Abraham Lincoln in 1865 and James A. Garfield in 1881.

The tomb sits on a bluff overlooking a park and the building that houses the McKinley Museum of History, Science and Industry. This is a wonderful museum that offers a glimpse not only into the life of William McKinley, but also into the industries and national firms that were either founded or have grown in Canton and affected our way of life. The newest addition is a hands-on discovery museum for youngsters of all ages that includes a life-size animated dinosaur, an electrical display that will really stand your hair on end, and a host of other interesting things for kids to see and do.

Mckinley Museum   (216) 455-7043
Discover World Children's Science Museum
800 McKinley Monument Drive, N.W.
Canton, Ohio 44708-4800   Handicapped access: yes

SOME BARGAIN BAKEWARE

Ekco Bakeware—those cooking pans you see in all the department stores—is made in nearby Massillon. On Tuesday and Thursday of each week the factory store is open to the public for a few hours, and you can buy new products as well as seconds and discontinued stock at a sizable savings. The only drawback is you have to be there between 10:30 a.m. and 2 p.m. on either Tuesday or Thursday. They accept only cash and take no credit cards.

Ekco Bakeware Factory Store   (216) 832-5026
359 State Avenue, Extension, N.W.
Massillon, Ohio 44648   Handicapped access: steps into plant

FRIED SPINACH LEAVES

That's just one of the unusual dishes offered at this family restaurant on Lincoln Way in Massillon. They are also famous for their sticky-buns, which servers keep offering as you eat your meal here. Lots of made-from-scratch dishes and wonderful desserts. Especially their strawberry pie!

D.D. Stutz Restaurant   (216) 477-2525
4508 Lincoln Way   Open seven days
Massillon, Ohio 44646   Handicapped access: yes

ONE OF MY FAVORITE BOOKSTORES

This newsstand has been a downtown Canton fixture for decades. Just about any magazine published can be found on the shelves, especially those dealing with sports and hobbies. They also have a well-stocked bookstore here and offer many volumes at bargain prices. I was especially happy to see the number of books they carry by Ohio authors, some published locally and very hard to find.

The News Depot   (216) 454-4441
207 North Market Street
Canton, Ohio 44702   Handicapped access: yes

CLASSIC CARS ON DISPLAY

This museum offers a look not only at the cars of the early part of this century, but also at the restoration work on some of the great old classics that are being readied for display. Included in the collection is a police car from the 1930s that has bullet-proof glass. The museum is small but very interesting to anyone interested in old cars.

Canton Classic Car Museum   (216) 455-3603
555 Market Street, South
Canton, Ohio 44702

THE FOOTBALL HALL OF FAME

Canton is the birthplace of professional football, and the home of the Pro Football Hall of Fame. Besides the busts of football heroes, uniforms of the great from past years of gridiron glory are on display, and you can match wits with football experts via interactive exhibits. The hall adds new members each August, and the ceremonies are held on the lawn in front of the football shrine. There is also a gift shop.

Pro Football Hall of Fame   (216) 456-8207
2121 George Halas Drive
Canton, Ohio 44708   Handicapped access: yes

THE FUMBLEBALL HALL OF FAME

There really is such a game and such a place. It is also right here in Canton.

Fumbleball is like softball and usually played by persons over the age of 35. There are only two leagues in the country, one in Canton, where a hall of fame has been established to honor its members.

Fumbleball Hall of Fame   (216) 453-1552
Greater Canton Amateur Sports Hall of Fame
1414 Market Ave., N.
Canton, Ohio 44708   Handicapped access: yes

A VACUUM CLEANER MUSEUM

The folks who make the Hoover Vacuum Cleaner have turned their founder's birthplace in North Canton into a museum for their machine. Included in the displays are cleaning devices that go back hundreds of years, as well as early Hoover prototypes. It's an interesting stop, especially on a rainy day.

Hoover Historical Center and Vacuum Cleaner Museum   (216) 499-0287
2225 Easton Street
North Canton, Ohio 44720   Handicapped access: steps to upper floors

A REAL OLD-FASHIONED ICE CREAM PARLOR

During the Football Hall of Fame festivities each year, you can usually find some of the football greats dropping into this Canton landmark, which has stood in the same spot for nearly 70 years. In fact you might even find initials from the 1930s carved in some of the tables.

What they serve here is real homemade ice cream, made the same way for nearly seven decades. The big seller is a dish made with three-quarters of a pound of vanilla ice cream, homemade chocolate syrup, and fresh-roasted pecans, all blended together and topped with a mound of whipped cream. It's called a "Bittner." No one seems quite sure how the name originated. It's believed that it was named for an early employee who developed the treat, which is served in a soda glass with a spoon.

Taggart's Ice Cream   (216) 452-6844
1401 Fulton Road, N.W.
Canton, Ohio 44703   Handicapped access: yes

From My Mailbag...

Mr. Zurcher,

My girlfriend and I went To ThaT non-elecTric bed and breakfast you wrote abouT. When we goT There we found They didn'T have any elecTric lighTs or indoor ToileTs. We had a Terrible Time. You should noT Tell abouT These places unless you explain ThaT non-elecTric means no lighTs!!

--LighTs ouT in New Philadelphia

12 My Adventures with Craig

WHEN MY SON, CRAIG, WAS about four years old I had an emergency. My wife had left for work, I was slated to make a One Tank Trip that day, and our baby-sitter called to say she was sick.

What was I going to do with my four-year-old son?

I took him with me.

I called videographer Ralph Tarsitano, whom we call "Tarts," explained my problem, and asked if he would object to Craig riding along with us. (I didn't bother to clear it with WJW-TV.)

Everything went fine on the shoot. Craig seemed to enjoy the attention he was getting by being the youngest member of a TV crew. It was Christmastime, and he was fascinated by the lights, the decorated store windows, and all the excitement.

A department store Santa Claus was sitting in a window talking to youngsters. Tarts had watched several kids press their noses against the window to watch, but by the time he got the camera in position the kids had wandered off. He pointed to Craig.

"Put him over by the window and let me get a shot of him watching Santa," he said.

I wasn't too sure.

"Uhhh, Tarts," I began, " I forgot to get clearance to bring Craig along."

"Nobody's gonna recognize him back at the station," Tarsitano replied as he motioned Craig into position. "Don't worry about it."

When Craig looked through the window his four-year-old eyes got as wide as pie plates as he beheld Santa Claus talking to the other youngsters.

I used the shot—just one of many in a pretty piece about Christmas coming to Chagrin Falls. A day later I was summoned to then-News Director Phyllis Quail's office.

"Was that your son Craig on that Christmas piece last night?" Phyllis asked.

I admitted that it was, but before I could begin my assurances that it was an emergency and that it would not happen again, she interrupted me.

"That was cute," she said. "You ought to take him with you more often. Our viewers like to see that we have families just like them."

I hastily agreed with her and said that, when possible, I would consider doing just that. At the same time I was mentally calculating how much I could also save in baby-sitting fees on days I traveled.

So, off and on, for the next 10 years, especially during school holidays and the summer, Craig became my partner on One Tank Trips. During those years he got to steer a real paddle-wheel boat down the Ohio River and ride in the fireman's seat of a steam-powered locomotive. He rode a jet-boat up the Niagara gorge. He took elephant rides and petted baby tigers. He watched the sun rise and set in different states. In short, he got to do things that many youngsters might only fantasize about.

But Craig never caught a fish.

I must confess I am not a fisherman, and throughout Craig's life I have taken him fishing probably fewer than a half-dozen times. When we visited the new Geneva State Park in Geneva-on-the-Lake a couple of years ago and a charter captain offered to take us where the really big fish were biting we jumped at the chance.

The boat was only about 19 feet long, and as we headed out into the lake, some four- to six-foot waves were beginning to roll. We bobbed around like a cork in a barrel as we pushed a mile or more out to the fishing grounds. When we reached the spot, Craig had to hang onto the rail with one hand as he cast his line with another.

Almost immediately he had a bite. Not only a bite, he had a big one on the line—it was almost bending his fishing rod in half. Then the fish began to run and the charter captain and crew began to shout advice to Craig:

"SNUG UP YOUR LINE!" shouted one.

"LET HIM RUN A BIT. BUT DON'T LET HIM BREAK THE LINE!" shouted another.

For the next 20 minutes, as the boat tossed and turned, Craig did his best to follow the shouted instructions, the fish getting closer and closer to the boat.

It was at this point that I noticed Craig's face was turning a light shade of green.

"Are you getting seasick?" I asked.

He just gave me a miserable look and nodded as he continued the battle to land the fish.

The captain and crew continued to call out advice until Craig suddenly handed the fishing rod to them and leaned over the rail, very sick.

Even with experienced fisherman on the line it still took several minutes to bring the near-record-sized walleye on board.

Craig, now pale and shaking, was sitting and looking into space as the captain held the fish by a gill and pushed it in front of his face.

"Look at that," declared the Captain, "it's just a half-inch short of a record."

Craig looked at the glassy-eyed, smelly fish a couple of inches from his nose and turned to hang over the rail again.

He stayed there most of the way into port. When we reached the dock the captain held up the fish again and asked if Craig wanted to clean it on the shore or pack it in ice to take home.

Craig, still a bit green around his own gills, said he didn't even want to look at that fish, or any other fish again as long as he lived.

The fish ended up going home with the captain and crew.

GENEVA STATE PARK

You can often find charter fishing captains at the concession stand at the marina. Marina officials can usually supply you with names and phone numbers of fishing guides.

This is also one of the state parks that offers the rent-a-camp program. If you and your family have never tried tenting or camping before, this is an easy and inexpensive way to try before you invest in all the expensive equipment.

For under $20 a night (rates vary at different parks) you can rent a large tent, complete with gasoline lantern, cookstove, cots, mattresses, ice cooler, picnic table, and fire-ring and firewood. In short, all you have to do is bring blankets and food.

Geneva State Park	(216) 466-8400 (Marina and park)
Route #1, PO Box 429	
Geneva, Ohio 44041	Handicapped access: yes

FRESH FRUIT

The area around Geneva and Geneva-on-the-Lake is rich farm land, and you can find many roadside markets offering grapes, apples, and peaches—for which the area is famous. You'll also find wineries that offer wine-tasting in their stores. Autumn is the best time to visit for these treats, although many places are open year-round.

If you like to pick your own apples or grapes, here are a couple of places we have stopped.

Brunsman Fruit Farm   (216) 466-1348
5729 North River Road (Route 307)
Geneva, Ohio 44041   Handicapped access: gravel driveways

Spring Hill Farm Market   (216) 466-7480
6062 South Ridge, West (Route 84)
Geneva, Ohio 44041   Handicapped access: yes

Old Firehouse Winery & Restaurant   (216) 466-9300
5499 Lake Road, Box 310
Geneva-on-the-Lake, Ohio 44041   Handicapped access: yes

OHIO'S OLDEST LAKE ERIE RESORT

That's the boast here at Geneva-on-the-Lake, which has been a vacation destination for folks since the mid-19th-century. They offer vacation cottages, a mini-amusement park, wineries, and restaurants. For more information contact:

Geneva-on-the-Lake Chamber of Commerce   (216) 466-8600
5536 Lake Road
Geneva-on-the-Lake, Ohio 44041

One Tank Tip #5
Coupon Clipper Alert
Check the local tourist and convention bureau for free or discount coupons for local attractions or restaurants and motels.

13 Romance and History

IF YOU ARE LOOKING FOR a romantic place to get away to for a weekend or just overnight, Elaine Crane, who operates Rider's Inn in Painesville, has just the answer.

For openers, the tavern has been around since the early 1800s providing shelter, food, and beverages for travelers. Today, while still maintaining a historic look, it offers modernized bedrooms with private baths and beautiful furnishings.

If you would like to surprise someone special, give the Inn a call and they can arrange for someone to go shopping and perhaps buy a slinky negligee or robe, in the right color and size, that will be on the bed waiting to be used when you arrive. Also, you can schedule a romantic dinner at the inn and, when you are finished eating, the hostess will offer to give you a tour of the premises. Upon reaching your room (which is the last stop on the tour), she hands you a key and gently closes the door leaving the two of you alone.

Rider's Inn   (216) 354-8200
792 Mentor Avenue
Painesville, Ohio 44077   Handicapped access: steps

A VERY SPECIAL MAILBOX

When I appear at places like the I-X Center in Cleveland, I usually have with me my special One Tank Trip Mail Box. It was made for me by the folks at The Mailbox Company, in Kirtland. The owner used to drive snowplows and had to repair mailboxes that he knocked over. He did such a good job that neighbors started asking him to build them a mailbox. Today he doesn't plow snow anymore, he builds mailboxes. Some look like homes, others like cars and trucks, still others resemble animals such as cows and pigs. Whatever your interest, the Mailbox Company can probably build a mailbox just for you.

The Mailbox Company   (216) 256-MAIL
7891 Chardon Road
Kirtland, Ohio 44092   Handicapped access: yes

FARMS AND RAILROADS

Lake Metroparks offers attractions based on farms and railroads and much, much more. For starters, at the Penitentiary Glen Park you can find a miniature steam railroad. A club, whose members build the steam trains, has its headquarters at the park, and, as a condition for using it, when they meet they give free rides on the little trains to kids and adults on a first-come, first-served basis.

Another wonderful attraction in Lake County is Lake Farmpark. Here you can wander around a barn, help milk a cow, crawl through a maze made of straw, or even take a horse-drawn hayride through the park. There are gift shops and even restaurants here.

Lake Metroparks offer many other attractions at properties throughout the county ranging from golf courses to wonderful waterfalls. Contact the park for maps and brochures.

Lake Farmpark   (216) 256-2122
8800 Chardon Road
Kirtland, Ohio 44094   Handicapped access: yes

Office: Lake Metroparks   (216) 639-7275
11211 Spear Road
Concord Township, Ohio 44077   Handicapped access: yes

A GARDEN CENTER TOUR

Lake County is one of the garden nursery centers of the country. The many large greenhouse complexes throughout the county make it a wonderful place to tour, especially in the spring.

One of the largest growers around is Champion Garden Towne in Perry. You can take a free tour of the place just by giving them a call. They also have a huge garden shop that carries just about anything you need for the garden. Open daily.

Champion Garden Towne   (216) 259-2811
3717 North Ridge Road (U.S. Route 20)
Perry, Ohio 44081   Handicapped access: yes

ZSA ZSA'S FAVORITE RESTAURANT

You never know when you might run into Zsa Zsa Gabor, of Hollywood fame, here at George's Famous Dinner Bell Restaurant in

Painesville Township. George Diskes, the owner, is a friend and confidant of Zsa Zsa's and has hosted her at the restaurant several times.

As for the "Famous" in the restaurant name, that's probably due to the huge portions that they serve here. Their soup has a hump in it, because they pile so much chicken and so many noodles into each bowl. This is also one of the few restaurants I have visited that offers prime rib, with eggs, for breakfast.

George's Famous Dinner Bell Restaurant   (216) 354-3708
1155 Bank Street
Painesville Township, Ohio 44077   Handicapped access: yes

OHIO'S PRESIDENTIAL TRAIL: JAMES A. GARFIELD

The 20th president of the United States made his home here in Mentor. Lawnfield is the twelve-room mansion where Garfield lived from 1876 until he was elected President in 1880, when he went to Washington, where he was assassinated just months after taking office.

At the time of this writing, the home is undergoing extensive restoration and is not expected to be completed until sometime in 1996. Other buildings on the property are being used in the meantime to house some of the Garfield memorabilia.

Lawnfield   (216) 255-8722
James A. Garfield Presidential Home
8095 Mentor Avenue
Mentor, Ohio   Handicapped access: steps in house

HOLDEN ARBORETUM

Lake County has the largest arboretum in the United States. With over 3,000 acres of land, Holden Arboretum contains woods, meadows, and ponds. It is a great place for birdwatchers. Wherever you go in the complex you find well-marked trails with signs identifying the various trees, wildflowers, and grasses. Especially beautiful in the spring and fall, Holden is nonetheless attractive year-round.

Holden Arboretum   (216) 946-4400
9500 Sperry Road
Mentor, Ohio 44060   Handicapped access: yes

14 Some People Fly, Some Don't

I WAS DRIVING WITH A camera crew on Cleveland's West Side when, crossing a bridge, we spotted what appeared to be a huge kite sailing over the valley near the steel plants. We went to investigate and, on top of a cliff near West 11th Street, we found a group of hangliding fans practicing their sport.

We watched for a while, did some filming of the event, and were preparing to leave when the leader, Chuck Slusarczyk, asked if I would like to try flying.

Now what they were doing was putting on a harness that was attached to a giant kite-shaped wing, hoisting it over their heads, running, and leaping off the edge of the cliff. Then, lifted by the wind, they would gently float and spiral down to a baseball diamond several hundred feet below in the valley.

Slusarczyk assured me that it was absolutely safe, that all you had to do was point the nose of the kite down to gain speed and point it up to slow or level out. Tip your body—hanging by the harness from the kite—to the right and you would turn right; tip left to turn left. The hardest part, he said, was carrying the kite back up the hill after you landed.

Apparently at this point I suffered a total loss of good sense and, egged on by photographers Dave Williams and Ted Pikturna, I somewhat reluctantly strapped on the hang glider. I found myself running pell-mell towards the edge of a cliff, hanging onto a huge kite with white knuckles.

Just as I stepped off the edge into space, I realized this was not the best idea that I had ever had.

The hang glider plummeted about 10 feet, and, as I was closing my eyes to avoid the impact with the earth below, I discovered that I was soaring.

It was like being a bird. I leaned to the right, and the hang glider went into a tight turn to the right. Unfortunately, I was too close to the edge of the cliff to turn, and I went slamming into a debris-littered slope. The impact dragged me over two discarded mattress springs and a patch of broken bottles before I stopped.

As I was counting my arms and legs to see if they were all there, Chuck Slusarczyk came sliding down the hillside.

"You turned too soon," he scolded me, as he helped me to my feet. "You go up there and try it again."

I looked down. My pants were in shreds, and a dozen cuts to my knees and shins were leaking blood into my shoes, and he wanted me to go again?

"No way!" I said.

"Come on, skin will grow back," Slusarczyk said. "Besides, if you don't go now, you'll be spooked and never try it again. You almost had it. Try it once more."

As I said, I was suffering from a total loss of common sense at the time, because a few minutes later I found myself on top of the hill shakily running again towards the edge of that same cliff.

This time I was expecting the sudden drop, and was determined to just soar straight across the valley to the baseball field. I attempted to slow the speed by raising the front of the hang-glider. It was too much and I began to stall! The hang-glider peeled off to the right and I found myself heading right back into the same patch of debris I had landed in on the first attempt.

I was still lying face down on a rusty bed spring when Slusarczyk and some friends reached me. My right pant leg was gone below the knee. I had bits and pieces of broken beer bottles embedded in my knees and shins, but otherwise I was unhurt.

My common sense had finally returned. Despite Slusarczyk's pleas that I try it one more time, I refused.

My photographers, Williams and Pikturna, suggested that I might want to go to a hospital to get the glass out of my legs and to get a tetanus shot.

They dropped me off at the emergency room at St. John Hospital and drove off to cover a fire while I was attended to.

Now, from the waist up I looked O.K. It was from the knees down where I was hurting, and since I was standing in front of her desk, the registrar could not see cuts on my legs.

"What's your problem?" she asked

"I'd like to see a doctor about patching up some cuts."

"How did you get hurt?" she said, not even looking up from the form she was filling out.

"Uh, I don't think you would understand," I replied.

"Try me," she said with some smugness, "I've heard just about everything."

"Okay," I said. "I fell off a kite."

"Sounds to me like you want a psychiatrist, instead of a medical doctor," she said.

You know, maybe she was right.

While I have never flown a hang glider again, I am still fascinated by flight and the men and women that have taken wing.

Each time I drive by the huge dirigible airdock at the old Akron City Airport, I am struck by the sheer size of the historic building. Opened in 1931, the airdock is 211 feet tall, 320 feet wide and 1,175 feet in length, without a single supporting pillar or girder. At the time, it was the largest such building in the world.

They say that you could lay out 10 football fields inside the structure, that the interior space is big enough to house two aircraft carriers, the Washington Monument, and the Statue of Liberty. The ceilings are so high that sometimes condensation causes small clouds to form inside the building.

It was constructed by the Goodyear Company of Akron to house their giant dirigibles, which nearly filled the airdocks. For an idea of how big the dirigibles were, today all of their active airships—or blimps—could fit in the space that just one dirigible once took up inside the airdock.

While no public tours are allowed of the inside of the building, it can easily be seen from surrounding roads and highways.

AN AKRON RITUAL

It's not officially spring until Strickland's ice cream stand opens. The homemade custard, made fresh each day, has been prepared from the same recipe for generations. Strickland's is right across the street from the old Akron Airport, and their parking lot is a good place to see the airdock while enjoying an ice-cream cone. Open seasonally, closed in winter.

Strickland's Frozen Custard
1809 Triplett Boulevard
Akron, Ohio 44303

A MUSEUM DEDICATED TO RUBBER

The Goodyear Rubber Company, which used to own the airdock, has a unique museum located in its office building downtown.

The World of Rubber devotes quite a bit of space to the dirigible era. There are lots of pictures of the airships, as well as pieces of an actual dirigible frame. The kids will like the open cockpit of a World War II Corsair fighter plane, manufactured by Goodyear—a great place to have your picture taken.

You can learn all about tires and rubber, and even see some really unusual products that were once made from rubber.

There is also a unique gift shop.

Goodyear World of Rubber Museum   (216) 796-2121
1201 East Market Street
Akron, Ohio 44316   Handicapped access: yes

STAN HYWET HALL AND GARDENS

The magnificent mansion owned by the Seiberling family, who owned Goodyear, is now open to the public. Its 60-some rooms range from the great hall to a wonderful music room, where Paderewski once played. There is an indoor swimming pool, game room, and formal gardens, which are a favorite with newlyweds for picture backgrounds. During the holidays, the mansion is decorated as it was during the time the Seiberling family lived there.

Stan Hywet Hall and Gardens   (216) 836-5533
714 North Portage Path
Akron, Ohio 44303   Handicapped Access: yes

ROUND HOTEL ROOMS

The only hotel in the world where you can sleep, in luxury, in a silo is at the Hilton Quaker Square Inn in Akron. The old cement silo complex, which once held the oats destined to become Quaker Oats Oatmeal, has been made into modern, round hotel rooms. The six-inch concrete walls guarantee privacy and quiet. The hotel also offers several restaurants and a night club. It is also attached to the Quaker Square shopping mall, which offers unique shops and specialty stores. You can even buy an oatmeal cookie fresh from the oven here.

Quaker Hilton Hotel   (216) 253-5970
Quaker Square, 135 South Broadway
Akron, Ohio 44313   Handicapped Access: yes

Cuyahoga Valley Railroad

AKRON TO CLEVELAND ON A TRAIN

You can actually take a train from Cleveland to Akron and vice versa. The Cuyahoga Valley Railroad has begun almost year-round trips from Independence, Ohio to downtown Akron. When the trains arrive in Akron, buses meet the train to carry the passengers to Quaker Square. On the way down, there is also a stop at the Western Reserve Historical Society's Hale Farm and Village in Bath, Ohio. You can get off the train and spend an afternoon there, then catch the train on its return later in the day to Cleveland.

There are plans to one day extend the train from Independence into downtown Cleveland.

The Cuyahoga Valley Railroad   (216) 657-2000
P.O. Box 158
Peninsula, Ohio 44264-0150   Handicapped access: steps into cars

WALK UNDER A POND

One of the best metroparks in Ohio is located in Akron. Here, you can walk beneath a mock-up of a farm pond and see pond life from a fish's point of view. This unique building also houses an observation room where, through one-way glass, you can watch wild animals while they feed just outside. The Summit County Metroparks also offer some truly great hiking trails in many of their other parks.

F.A. Seiberling Naturealm   (216) 836-2185
1828 Smith Road
Akron, Ohio 44313
or

Summit County Metroparks   (216) 867-5511
975 Treatyline Road
Akron, Ohio 44313   Handicapped access: yes

A TOMBSTONE JUST ISN'T A TOMBSTONE ANYMORE

You can take a tour of the North Hill Marble and Granite Company. While most of the business still consists of making tombstones, they also find other uses for their talents to serve the living. They offer a really different way to identify your home: a large boulder inscribed with the family name and street number as well as a duck, perhaps, or symbol of a favorite hobby or sport. They also offer small inscribed stones for gardens with poems and quotations.

Getting back to the tombstone business, they also specialize in tombstones for pets. The largest they have ever done was a tombstone for a horse.

North Hill Marble and Granite Company   (216) 253-2179
448 North Howard Street
Akron, Ohio 44310   Handicapped access: steps in building

SLEIGH RIDES AND CARRIAGE RIDES

When snow is on the ground, you can have a never-to-be-forgotten experience: a sleigh ride in an authentic cutter, pulled by a horse in a harness festooned with bells. It's like a scene from a Currier and Ives print.

The owner, Wade Johnson, builds his own sleighs, which are modern replicas of the famous 19th-century "one horse open sleighs." The rides are taken at his farm and the paths run over hills and through woods, just like in the song. In fact, he even encourages his passengers to sing.

When the ride is over you are invited back to his carriage barn for hot cappuccino and some sweets around the potbellied stove in his carriage museum.

During warmer weather, when there is no snow, Johnson also has beautiful carriages that provide rides and picnics at nearby Brandywine Falls in the Cuyahoga Valley National Recreation Area. Reservations are always required.

Carriage Trade   (216) 650-6262 (Akron) (216) 467-9000 (Cleveland)
8050 Brandywine Road
Northfield, Ohio 44067   Handicapped access: yes

A WINTER SPORTS PARADISE

If you like sledding, cross-country skiing, or snowshoeing, you can find all three at the Virginia Kendall Park, operated by the National Park Service. In fact, if you do not own a pair of snowshoes, the park rangers will lend you a pair, free. All you have to do is leave your driver's license. At special times, Rangers who are expert on snowshoes will lead visitors on snowshoe walks through the woods and around the lake on winter nature walks. These are also free. Call for times. The sledding hills and cross-country ski trails are open whenever weather permits.

Virginia Kendall Park   (216) 526-5256 or 1-(800) 433-1986
Cuyahoga Valley National Recreation Area
15610 Vaughn Road
Brecksville, Ohio 44141

15 You Never Know About Those TV People

WE HAD SET UP A BOOTH at the annual outdoor sports and travel show at the giant I-X Center to hand out our One Tank Trips Booklets to visitors.

It was about the end of the fifth day that I had been there when a friend, Lieutenant J. P. Allen of the Ohio State Patrol, stopped by. J.P. looks like a recruiting poster for the State Highway Patrol—six-foot-one, sandy-haired, handsome. He was off-duty and wearing a flannel shirt and dungarees. I invited him to join me in the booth so we could chat in between visits by viewers.

We had been talking about ten minutes when I got rather busy with several people who had questions. J. P. stood beside me watching the crowd when he noticed an elderly lady studying him.

She would look first at J. P. then study the pictures on the back of the booth. We had posted large color photographs of all of our leading anchors: Tim Taylor, Dick Goddard, Casey Coleman, and Tana Carli. Tana, from Alliance, had been a runner-up for the title of Miss America and was the first female evening anchor hired by TV8.

The lady stood for several minutes looking first at the pictures and then at J.P. Finally she stepped up to the counter.

"Which one are you?" she said, nodding toward the wall of pictures.

"Oh, I'm Tana Carli," he said, jokingly.

"No you're not," the woman declared. "You're a man."

The challenge in the woman's voice was just enough to trigger J.P.'s sense of humor.

"Yes, I am Tana Carli," he replied, moving back to stand beside Tana's picture.

"That's impossible," said the woman again. "You're a man."

"Take a good look and use your imagination," J.P. pleaded, as he held Tana's picture up beside his head. "Picture me with a woman's wig, false eyelashes and some makeup, and wearing a dress."

J.P. smiled at the lady with his best Tana Carli smile.

She stared at J.P. and the picture, her face showing confusion.

"But you're a good-looking man, why would you want to dress up like a woman?" the lady finally blurted.

"Well, it's this way. I wanted to get into television, but they didn't have any openings for men at the time, and so I decided to apply as a woman," he answered, with a straight face.

The lady still wasn't totally buying his story.

"If you're Tana Carli let's hear you say something like she says it," she challenged.

Without batting an eye, J.P. raised Tana's picture in front of his face and said, in a falsetto voice:

"The attack of killer parakeets; next on Newscenter 8."

Now, J.P. does not sound a bit like Tana Carli, but the power of suggestion must have been at work as he held the picture in front of his face because the woman's mouth dropped open and she exclaimed:

"MY GOD! You really are her!"

From behind the picture J.P. gave me a wink.

"I just can't believe this is really true," the woman continued.

I was struck by a fit of coughing and excused myself from the counter.

J.P. was just warming up.

"Did you like that sweater I was wearing on the news show last night?" he asked the woman.

"Uh, yes," the lady replied. "It was quite attractive."

"I bought that at Value City," he said. "I just love bargains, don't you?"

The more they talked, the more convinced the lady became that J.P. was indeed Tana Carli.

Finally an elderly man, obviously the woman's husband, wandered up to the booth.

"You ready to go yet?" he asked her.

"You're never going to believe who this man is," the woman gushed at her husband.

Before he could guess, she blurted out:

"This is Tana Carli, on TV 8!"

"Go on!" Her husband responded.

"No, really," she said. "He wears a wig and a dress when he's on television."

"Woman, have you lost your mind!" he retorted.

The woman turned to a smiling J.P. and pleaded:

"Put the picture in front of your face and talk to him like Tana," she said.

So J.P. complied, and, again, the power of suggestion apparently overcame reason as the man stepped back, studied J.P., and said,

"I'll be damned!"

As the couple wandered off, still shaking their heads we could hear the man telling the wife

"You just never know about those TV people."

INDOOR FERRIS WHEEL

The huge, sprawling I-X Center was built on the edge of Cleveland Hopkins International Airport during World War II. At times it has served as a bomber and tank plant, turning out weapons of war for both WWII and Korea.

In recent years it has been turned into the largest exhibition hall in the country. Here is an illustration of just how big it is. When the Republicans were considering the I-X Center for their national convention, it was pointed out that the President could pull Air Force One—the presidential aircraft—right inside it.

In fact, there are 20 acres under one roof here, and one of the more unique ways this space is used is as an indoor amusement park each spring. The 10-story-high Ferris Wheel stays year-round and is used when other shows are running at the center. The Ferris Wheel, which pops through the roof, is the largest indoor Ferris Wheel in the world.

I-X Center   (216) 676-6000
6200 Riverside Drive
Cleveland, Ohio 44135   Handicapped access: yes

ASTRONAUT ICE CREAM

At the other end of Cleveland Hopkins International Airport you will find the NASA Lewis Research Center. The visitor center offers an interesting look into the work being done here, as well as exhibits tracing the history of airplanes and space flight. There is also a nice gift shop in the visitor center where you can buy space souvenirs, including Astronaut Ice Cream. It's dried ice cream that has a plastic appearance, yet when you place it in your mouth it tastes just like the real thing.

Visitor Center, Lewis Research Center, NASA   (216) 267-1187
21000 Brookpark Road
Cleveland, Ohio 44135   Handicapped Access: yes

THE CLEVELAND METROPARKS

Also bordering Cleveland Hopkins International Airport is part of the Cleveland Metroparks system. The Rocky River Reservation offers picnicking, fishing, bridal trails and stables, golf, baseball diamonds, sledding hills, all-persons trails, a marina, and a great place to just relax on a nice day. It's all part of the "Emerald Necklace" chain of metroparks surrounding Cleveland.

Cleveland Metroparks   (216) 351-6300
4101 Fulton Parkway
Cleveland, Ohio 44144   Handicapped access: yes

From My Mailbag...

Dear Mr. Zurcher,

Please send me everything you know. I have enclosed a self-addressed stamped envelope.

P.S. Please let me know if you need more than one stamp.

16 A Real Human Fly

"OUR COMPANY SOLD SEVERAL of them to Buckingham Palace in England," the man on the telephone declared.

"A personal fire escape system?" I replied.

"That's right," the salesman responded. "If your bedroom is above the first floor you ought to have one of these."

When the man offered to come to Cleveland to give a demonstration by climbing down the front of a downtown building, I agreed to do a story on his product.

A week later Charles Morgan arrived at our studios. He had some bad news; his arm was in a sling. Due to a sprained wrist, he would be unable to demonstrate the personal fire escape for me. But not to worry, he said, "This system is so easy to use that one of the princes at the Palace uses it to sneak out of his room. Why don't you try it?"

"I get nosebleeds when I stand on a chair," I pointed out.

"All you have to do is sit in this sling," he said, "and hang onto this rope. Just feed it out at the speed you want to be lowered to the ground."

He was holding up a series of rather sturdy-looking ropes and a wide canvas belt. The idea, he said, was to go up on the roof of our four-story building and find a suitable place to tie the ropes, then place the canvas sling around my rear end and just step over the edge and lower myself to the ground.

Shortly, I found myself standing on the roof of the TV studio. The ropes had been tied to an iron pipe, snaked over the sandstone ledge, and draped down the building side to Euclid Avenue.

My first concern came when I noticed Morgan looking at an instruction book that came with the fire escape. A puzzled look now and then flitted across his face.

"Are you sure this is really safe?" I asked, as I looked over the edge of the roof and felt butterflies grow in my stomach when I realized how far down four stories could really be.

"Oh, absolutely!" he replied, "Our ropes are one hundred percent guaranteed. If one should ever break, for any reason, we replace it, without charge to you."

I was just about to ask what good a new rope was going to do me if I fell four stories when I noticed a demonstration down on the street. Videographer Ralph Tarsitano, who had been assigned to film my descent had organized a group of bystanders, who were chanting:

"Jump! Jump! JUMP!"

Tarsitano, seeing me peering over the edge of the roof, shouted up:

"Hey! Would you mind either climbing down here, or jumping. It's just about time to go to lunch!"

Back on the roof, Morgan was nervously strapping me into the harness. I noticed his hands were shaking. Just then our General Manager, Chuck Bergeson, strode onto the scene.

"You don't have to do this!" he said sternly. "Just remember you don't have to do this and if you get hurt there won't be any worker's compensation."

With that, he whirled and stomped off.

With all of this support I felt I just had to try it. I carefully pulled the rope taut and sat down on the edge of the roof. The chanting, "Jump! Jump!", was still going on, with Tarsitano now leading it.

I closed my eyes and pushed off. I swung out then slammed back into the brick building. I wasn't going anywhere. I was just hanging there!

"You've got to let go of the rope so it will pay out the line!" shouted Morgan from above me, still holding the instruction book.

I timidly let go of the rope and dropped immediately almost six feet before I again snatched the rope in a death grip and my descent was checked.

I now found myself hanging between the top of the building and the windows on the third floor. I opened one eye and could see fellow workers behind the windows waving at me. I weakly smiled at them and then looked down. It was a big mistake. The bottom of the Grand Canyon would have appeared closer than the street, three stories below me.

A brisk wind was now whistling down Euclid Avenue and I began to swing on my perch, blown back and forth by the breeze. The word "terrified" would not adequately describe my feelings at that moment.

"PAY OUT THE ROPE!" Morgan was shouting from the roof, still clutching the instruction book.

Inch by inch I let the rope slide through my hands, suddenly realizing that I could control the rate of my descent down the building. I had just reached the level of the top of the first floor windows when Morgan leaned over and shouted something that I could not understand.

He was still shouting something as my trembling legs touched the sidewalk and I half-collapsed against the side of the building. I was greeted by a spattering of applause from bystanders. I was still standing there when Morgan burst through the front door, still clutching the instruction book. His face was white as a sheet.

"Are you all right?" he gasped

"Yeah, I'm fine," I replied. "What where you trying to tell me as I got near the bottom?"

"That the rope was breaking!" he responded.

It turned out Morgan had never actually used the harness himself and it was the first time he had ever had someone demonstrate it. When we strung the ropes over the edge of the sandstone at the top, he forgot to put a rubber pad between the rope and the stone. The result was that every time I swung back and forth on the rope it grated across the sandstone lip, cutting the rope. Only a few strands of nylon still held it together as I reached the sidewalk. Next time, I think I'll just take the elevator.

MY FAVORITE CLEVELAND THINGS

I am often asked for my favorite attractions in Cleveland. The problem is there are so many. So I have tried to boil it down to a few that I always show to visitors from out of town.

THE TERMINAL TOWER

While it no longer holds the title of Cleveland's tallest building (Society Tower now has that honor), I still get a thrill from the view atop Cleveland's landmark. If you have never taken the elevator ride to the top, or looked down on Public Square, or enjoyed the 360-degree view of Cleveland that pigeons see every day, you have missed a real experience. For more than 60 years the sight of this office tower has spelled "Welcome" to visitors from all over the world and especially to Clevelanders returning home. The 42nd-floor observation deck is open on weekends only.

Terminal Tower Observation Deck   (216) 621-7981
50 Public Square
Cleveland, Ohio 44101   Handicapped access: yes

A BIG CORNED BEEF SANDWICH

Rave all you want about your Chicago corned beef sandwiches. I say Cleveland is the Corned Beef Capital of America. Just drive through the downtown area and count the number of diners and small eating places that specialize in the briny brisket.

A tiny restaurant on St. Clair is where I usually go to satisfy my cravings for the salty red meat. Here, they carve it thin and pile it high on fresh rye bread—almost four inches high. Then they slather it with mustard and pile on a heaping tablespoon of some potent horseradish. My eyes water at the memory of this lunchtime treat.

Danny's Deli   (216) 696-1761
1658 St. Clair Avenue
Cleveland, Ohio 44103   Handicapped access: step into restaurant, narrow crowded aisles

THE U.S.S. COD

There aren't too many Great Lakes states that have a submarine parked on their waterfront. The U.S.S. Cod was a fighting ship in World War II. After her wartime service she was brought to Cleveland to be used by the Navy Reserve for training. When she was declared surplus and it looked like the submarine would be scrapped, a citizens' group was formed and funds were raised to have her made into a floating museum with a permanent home on Cleveland's lakefront.

The sub has been kept in original World War II condition. That means to get in and out you have to squeeze through hatches and climb up and down ladders just like the crew did more than 50 years ago. It's not an ideal place for skirts and high-heeled shoes.

U.S.S. Cod   (216) 566-8770
The Great Lakes Historical Society, 1089 East 9th Street
Cleveland, Ohio 44114
Handicapped access: Ramp to deck. Narrow hatches and ladders into submarine

EDGEWATER STATE PARK

The 100-acre park that sits on Cleveland's front step is one of my favorite spots to take visitors for a view of the Cleveland skyline. From an outlook called Perkins Beach on the western end of the park (accessible from the shoreway), you can see one of most impressive views of Cleveland, with tall buildings spiking into the sky. In the foreground, rolling waves hit the shore of Edgewater State Park. The park offers swimming, boating, exercise trails, fishing, and even kite-flying areas. It's one of the city's favorite playgrounds.

Edgewater State Park
Cleveland Lakefront State Park, 6700 Memorial Shoreway
Cleveland, Ohio 44147   Handicapped access: yes

LAKE VIEW CEMETERY

Out-of-town friends are usually taken aback when I suggest we visit a cemetery. But Lake View Cemetery isn't your average burial ground. It started out as an arboretum and still has an impressive display of trees and flowers in the springtime. It is also the final resting spot of President James A. Garfield, tycoon John D. Rockefeller, inventor Charles Brush, and many other notables of Cleveland's—and the nation's—past. Cemetery officials actually encourage visitors to walk, hike, even picnic in the cemetery.

Lake View Cemetery   (216) 421-2665
12316 Euclid Avenue
Cleveland, Ohio 44106   Handicapped access: yes

THE CUYAHOGA COUNTY ARCHIVES

This interesting old building is the repository of all of the county records. Here you can find a description of Elliot Ness's apartment when he lived on Lake Avenue and a copy of George Burns and Gracie Allen's marriage license (they were married here while appearing at Play House Square). There are gruesome pictures of Kingsbury Run murder victims from the coroner's old files. If you are looking into your family's history, they have records dating back to the founding of the city—back when a bounty was paid by the county commissioners for killing wolves. It's a fun place to spend a rainy day.

Cuyahoga County Archives   (216) 443-7250
2905 Franklin Avenue
Cleveland, Ohio 44113   Handicapped access: steps into building, narrow aisles

ALADDIN'S BAKERY

Have you ever wondered how pita bread is made with a pocket? Well, wonder no more. Just take a tour of Aladdin's Bakery. You can watch as the pitas come from the oven, looking like small basketballs, to be pressed flat by packers. Aladdin's is also a great place to sample some middle-eastern foods like falafel, tabbouleh, and, of course, pita bread.

Aladdin's Bakery   (216) 861-0317
1301 Carnegie Avenue
Cleveland, Ohio 44115   Handicapped access: yes

LOLLY THE TROLLEY

Even if you have lived in Cleveland all of your life and know every side of the city, I think you will be surprised at what you learn on one of Lolly the Trolley's tours of Cleveland. The driver-guides are not only very personable, but also very knowledgeable and will give you some new insights into the town. It's fun for strangers and residents alike. You can find Lolly at Burke Lakefront Airport and the Powerhouse in the Flats. For reservations call:

Lolly the Trolley   (216) 771-4484
1831 Columbus Road
Cleveland, Ohio 44113   Handicapped access: steps into trolley.

One Tank Tip #6
Good Timing Pays Off

When possible try to travel in the off-season winter and early spring months, for bargain prices and a better choice of hotels and motels.

17 Ohio's Presidential Trail: Fremont

AFTER THE STATE OF VIRGINIA, Ohio has a record number of native sons who became president of the United States. They came from just about every corner of the Buckeye state, starting with a transplanted Virginian, William Henry Harrison, in North Bend, Ohio, near the Ohio-Indiana border, and ending with Warren G. Harding of Marion. In between there was Civil War Hero U. S. Grant, born in Point Pleasant, at the bottom of the state, and James Garfield of Mentor. There was also William Howard Taft of Cincinnati, and William McKinley of Niles and Canton. Benjamin Harrison was the grandson of William Henry Harrison and was born at his grandfather's farm in North Bend. The president who is possibly the least known, but who left perhaps the biggest legacy to the state of Ohio, is Rutherford B. Hayes.

Rutherford B. Hayes, known as "Rudd" to his friends, had a distinguished record as congressman, governor of Ohio, and Civil War general. He was elected to the presidency in a disputed election that saw the outcome decided by an electoral commission. Hayes pledged not to run for re-election. In his inaugural address he summed up his feelings with these words: "He serves his party best, who serves his country best."

Hayes was credited with helping bind up the wounds of the Civil War by ending the rule of carpetbaggers in the South. He also rooted out corruption in government and helped establish the civil service.

When he was done with his one term, he came back to Ohio, to Spiegelgrove, his home in Fremont. Here he lived out the rest of his life. His son, Medal of Honor-winner Col. Webb Hayes, built a library to his father's memory on the estate grounds; it was the first presidential library in American history.

Today the Hayes Presidential Center in Fremont honors not only President Hayes but also all the men who have served as the nation's chief executive. In the museum there are exhibits honoring each of the presidents.

The beautiful Victorian mansion where Hayes lived is also kept as it was in his day and is open to the public.

President and Mrs. Hayes were buried on the estate. His grave is covered with a simple stone that has only his name. There is no mention that he once was a general, governor, and president of the United States.

Rutherford B. Hayes Presidential Center   (800) 998-7737
1337 Hayes Avenue
Fremont, Ohio 43420   Handicapped access: yes

Hayes Home

OTHER THINGS TO DO IN FREMONT

Scuba diving in a quarry is one of the things you can do in the Sandusky County Park System in and around Fremont. At White Star Park there is a bathing beach and an abandoned quarry that is filled by clear spring water, which, according to divers, makes this one of the better places in northern Ohio for practicing dives.

Wolf Creek Park offers camping along a winding river not far from Fremont.

Sandusky County Park District   (419) 334-4495
1970 Countryside Drive
Fremont, Ohio 43420   Handicapped Access: yes

FACTORY OUTLET SHOPPING

Fremont is also home to several industries, including one that makes infant clothes. They have a factory store specializing in baptismal and confirmation gowns and clothes for infants up to 24 months. It is open to the public each Wednesday for just five hours, from 10:00 a.m. until 3:00 p.m.

Infant Items, Inc.
Factory Outlet
1071 North Fifth Street
Fremont, Ohio 43420
(419) 332-7361
Handicapped access: yes

SHOPPING AT THE PRESIDENTIAL CENTER

Don't overlook the bargains to be had at the Hayes Presidential Center. Rare books from the library are often on sale, as well as limited-edition Christmas ornaments and several one-of-a-kind items for history buffs.

Hayes Presidential Center Museum Shop   1-(800) 998-7737
1337 Hayes Avenue
Fremont, Ohio 43420   Handicapped access: yes
No admission charge to enter museum store

One Tank Tip #7
Mid-Week Travel Can Be Easier
When possible try to travel mid-week. You will usually find a better selection of rooms available as well as shorter lines at popular attractions than on weekends.

18 Sandusky Bay

I HAD THE OPPORTUNITY a couple of years back to see San-dusky Bay from a point of view usually reserved for birds.

Some friends suggested that I try parasailing. That's riding a para-chute attached to a boat, which tows the chute with you hanging from beneath it—the chute, not the boat.

I had seen all these videotapes of poor, misguided middle-aged men and women who had been talked into a similar ride. You see them running as fast as they can on a beach as a speedboat heads for deep water. A long rope tied to the person on the shore gets taut and then slams them, face first, into the sand and drags them through the water.

"That's not for me," I told my friend.

"We don't do it that way," he insisted. "It's just like sitting in a rock-ing chair, only one that flies 300 feet in the air over the lake."

So, on a sunny morning I found myself with videographer Bob Begany in the back of a strange-looking speedboat on Sandusky Bay. The rear of the boat was covered with a large square platform. I was told to put on a life jacket and a harness and to sit on the plat-form.

The boat sped up and a crew member unfurled a huge parachute off the rear of the boat. Tow straps attached to two stantions held the parachute down.

Once it was filled with air, the crew member motioned for me to step up to the stantions and told me to grab the straps. As I did, he transferred the snaps from the stantions to my harness.

Before I had time to ask what to do next, I felt myself suddenly lifted into the air by the parachute. An electric winch began to pay out line, letting me go higher and higher as the boat picked up speed.

I soon found myself floating hundreds of feet over Lake Erie, the boat now looking like some small water bug dashing across the lake below me.

It was very pleasant up there. I could even seen the distant Cana-dian shoreline. I was still clinging to the straps above my head with a white-knuckle grip, but I was beginning to relax and almost enjoy the trip when I noticed that I was starting to sink towards the water.

The boat was heading into the wind and was unable to keep up enough speed to keep me in the air, and I was slowly floating closer and closer to the surface of Lake Erie.

I was ready to take a deep breath before hitting the water when I stopped going down and seemed to just hover over the surface of the water. My feet occasionally touched a wave, as the boat gained enough speed to keep me floating just over the surface.

The boat turned and started running away from the wind, and I soared back into the sky. This time I noticed, as we rose higher and higher away from the roar of the boat's motor, that all I could hear was the creak of the nylon harness stretching and making strange noises as it adjusted to the pull of the rope and to my weight. I began to get a mental image of what it would be like if the harness suddenly broke and I dropped 200 feet to the water below. It made me grab the straps all the more tightly over my head!

A few minutes later I felt myself starting to lower again, but this time I was being reeled in by the rope and I was headed towards the boat, not the water. In seconds I gently stepped down onto the surface of the boat, and the crew member quickly tied the chute onto the stantions, releasing me.

I was more than a little proud of myself for having taken such a daring ride, and looked to the young crew member expecting him to congratulate me on being so cool on my roller coaster—style ride, when he turned and said:

"You were a bit nervous up there. Last week I had an 85-year-old lady up celebrating her birthday. You should have seen her," he said with admiration. "She insisted on taking her camera with her. She shot three rolls of film and changed film in the camera twice while she was up there."

North Coast Parasail   (419) 627-2279
Oceana Midway Beach, Cedar Point
Sandusky, Ohio 44871   Handicapped access: sandy beach to boat

CRUISE TO THE ISLANDS

A wonderful way to see Sandusky Bay and the Lake Erie Islands is to take one of the many cruise boats that offer day-long cruises through the bay and around the islands, stopping at several before heading back to Sandusky that evening.

Goodtime I Cruises   (419)-625-9692
Jackson Street Pier
Sandusky, Ohio   Handicapped access: yes
Mailing address: 1006 East Strub Road, Sandusky, Ohio 44870

MERRY-GO-ROUND MUSEUM

This is one of Sandusky's newest attractions. The old post office building, with its rotunda, has been turned into a carousel museum featuring an actual working merry-go-round and exhibits of carousel horses and figures from around the world. There are also demonstrations by a carver who makes and repairs the horses. A gift shop is also on the premises. Tours are available and you can also ride the merry-go-round. Open year-round.

Merry-go-round Museum   (419) 626-6111
Corner West Washington & Jackson Streets, P.O. Box 718
Sandusky, Ohio 44870   Handicapped access: yes

HISTORIC JOHNSON ISLAND

During the Civil War, Confederate officers were imprisoned on an island in Sandusky Bay. Some escaped, while others died or were killed here. Today, a Confederate cemetery and a statue of a Confederate soldier are all that remain of this tragic chapter in Sandusky Bay's history. The cemetery is open to visitors and can be reached by boat or by causeway from the mainland.

Confederate Cemetery
Johnson Island
Sandusky Bay

A BIG ICE-CREAM CONE

Toft's Dairy of Sandusky is an institution. Generations of Sanduskians have made a pilgrimage to this dairy store on a summer's day for a single, double, or triple ice-cream cone. Newcomers get a real surprise. Their "single" is really two large dips of ice cream; there are three dips for a "double"; and a triple—well, you have to have a milk-shake cup to keep all the dips upright on the ice cream cone. It's a true ice-cream lover's kind of place.

Toft's Dairy and Ice Cream   (800) 521-4606
3717 Venice Road (Route 6)
Sandusky, Ohio 44870   Handicapped access: yes

AN ESTATE WINERY

A small farm market and estate winery that has won gold medals for its wine-making is located on the outskirts of Sandusky. Here you can find unusual wines like "Black Pearl," made with special grapes developed in the winery's vineyards.

The market also sells unusual items like buffalo stew, black popcorn, and fresh apple fritters.

Steuk's Winery and Market   (419) 625-0803
1001 Fremont Avenue (Route 6)
Sandusky, Ohio 44870   Handicapped access: yes

FISH DINNERS

The local folks have a couple of favorite taverns where they enjoy fresh Lake Erie perch dinners. The decor at each is basic "neighborhood bar," but the folks are friendly and the food is good.

Vickie's Restaurant and Bar   no phone number provided
902 West Adams Street
Sandusky, Ohio 44878   Handicapped access: yes

East Side Cafe   (419) 627-1964
1319 First Street
Sandusky, Ohio 44878   Handicapped access: steps into building

FLYING OVER THE BAY

Griffing Flying Service has been providing a lifeline year-round
to the folks on the Lake Erie islands for at least two generations. They
fly in freight and serve as an airborne ambulance when someone is
ill and needs to go to a mainland hospital. They take many people on
their first flight—home from the hospital—and, sadly, some of the
islanders on their last flight when they die.

The airline offers both regularly scheduled island flights and
charter flights over the entire Sandusky Bay area.

Griffing Flying Service   (419) 626-5161
3115 Cleveland Road
Sandusky, Ohio 44870   Handicapped access: yes

BEST MILK SHAKE

One of the best milk shakes I've had in recent years can be found
in a most unusual place: the snack bar here at Griffing Flying Service's Sandusky Airport. They make it with several dips of ice cream
and they test it by standing a straw up straight. If the straw leans,
they put in more ice cream.

Snack Bar, Griffing Flying Service   (419) 626-5161
3115 Cleveland Road
Sandusky, Ohio 44870   Handicapped access: yes

19. **The Island**

WHOP! WHOP! WHOP!

Whop! Whop! Whop!

Through my closed eyelids I could see the shadow of the propeller as it flashed over my head. It was like the opening scene of Apocalypse Now, except this was not a movie—this was real, and I was lying on my back on a small island while a real helicopter hovered just a few feet above me.

What had brought me to Starve Island, a tiny spit of sand jutting out of Lake Erie off South Bass Island, was the idea that videographer Bill West and I had cooked up to emphasize the joys of an island One Tank Trip. Starve Island is about 30 feet long and 6 feet wide. We pictured a final shot that would show me sleeping in the sun and then, as the helicopter lifted higher and higher, would reveal me on a private island in the middle of Lake Erie.

Helicopter pilot Andy Overley had outfitted his craft with pontoons for this shoot, and we waited until late afternoon when the sun would be in just the right position. It looked like everything was going to work perfectly. We circled the tiny island a couple of times before starting down. We noticed several seagulls take off, but gave them little thought. Andy was more concerned with the number of rocks sticking up at uneven angles. He finally decided that it would not be possible to set down on the island, but that he could hover just a foot or so off the rocks. I could sit in the doorway and just step out, and when I got in position, he would then lift straight up.

The downdraft from the helicopter blades set up a veritable whirlwind of feathers and sand as we sat hovering over the rocks. I shielded my eyes from the wind and quickly stepped out and lay down on the greenish rocks with a child's innertube beneath my head for a pillow. I heard the "Whop! Whop! Whop!" of the blades as Andy applied more power to lift off. I peeked out of one eye and could see the lens on Bill West's video camera two feet away from my face and starting to lift away.

As the helicopter soared into the sky and the wind from the propellers lessened I became aware of some new sensations. The rock was wet and slippery. It also smelled. Just then I heard it: the sound of angry sea gulls! Opening both eyes I saw the sky above me filled with seagulls. I was lying in the middle of a smelly seagull rookery, and around me were several nests! I scrambled to my feet and frantically waved at the helicopter, which was now wandering 2,000 feet in the air along the edge of South Bass Island. We had agreed that when they took off Andy and Bill would then shoot the outline of the bigger islands before coming back to retrieve me.

For the next 15 minutes I used the small plastic innertube and my hat to scare off angry gulls that kept zooming in closer and closer, scolding me with their raspy voices. I also realized that my back, from head to toe, was covered in slimy bird dung. It was just about the longest 15 minutes of my life!

Finally, the helicopter came back and I clawed my way back inside, much to the amusement of pilot Overley and videographer West—amusement until the smell of my guano-soaked clothes intensified in the heat of the helicopter's bubble cockpit. We then made a high-speed run to the nearest landing strip in Port Clinton.

Bird droppings aside, the Lake Erie islands make a wonderful place for a getaway for the weekend, a week, or all summer—and winter, too.

SOUTH BASS ISLAND

The Perry Peace Monument on South Bass Island, 352 feet high, dominates the skyline. From the observation platform at its top, on a clear day, you can see the Canadian shoreline. Park rangers will point out where Commodore Oliver Hazard Perry defeated the British Fleet during the War of 1812. The monument also serves as a grave marker for British seamen whose bodies washed ashore after the battle.

Besides all the history, the memorial is also a great spot for viewing all the islands.

Perry Victory and International Peace Memorial   (419) 285-2184
Bayview Avenue, P.O. Box 78
Put-In-Bay, Ohio 43456   Handicapped access: yes

PERRY'S CAVE

Legend has it that Commodore Perry stored ammunition in this 52-foot-deep cave on the island. A natural limestone cavern, it is open during summer months for tours.

Perry's Cave   (419) 285-2405
Catawba Street
Put-in-Bay, Ohio 43456

WINERY AND CAVE

Heineman Winery, right across the street from the Perry Cave, has its own cave as a tourist attraction. The difference is that Crystal Cave has the world's largest celestite crystals. It is unlike any cave you have ever been in. Upstairs, in the winery and garden, you can sample some of the famous island wines.

Heineman Winery and Vineyards   (419) 285-2811
Crystal Cave, Catawba Street
Put-In-Bay, Ohio 43456

WINTERTIME ON THE ISLAND

There is a second tourist season here: wintertime. That's when ice fishing attracts hundreds to the vastness of a frozen Lake Erie. Many of the island's summertime fishing guides also are experts on ice fishing and provide little heated shacks and transportation onto the ice to catch some trophy walleyes. A guide we have used in summer and winter is:

Pat Chrysler, Fishing Guide   (419)285-4631
Put-in-Bay, Ohio 43456

AN ISLAND WITH A SLOWER PACE

Kelley's Island is the largest American island in the waters of Lake Erie. Tourism is just being discovered here. It's a favorite with families because of its state park, its famous glacial grooves, left by the last ice age, and the recent development of some very nice bed and breakfasts.

FLY INN BED AND BREAKFAST

This new building offers perhaps some of the most luxurious and modern rooms on the island. Some of the bedrooms have private baths and one even has a whirlpool tub. They also offer a swimming pool for the kids and—get this—the place is located right on the airfield. That means the airplane that brings you to the island can pull right off the runway to the front door! The owner is also a pilot with his own plane and offers a package weekend that includes a sightseeing flight around the islands.

Fly Inn Bed and Breakfast   (419) 746-2525
Dwelle Lane, P.O. Box 471
Kelley's Island, Ohio 43438   Handicapped access: yes

A VICTORIAN BED AND BREAKFAST

They offer a romantic touch here. Fly into the island airport and a horse-drawn carriage awaits to take you and your bags to this Victorian farmhouse. This building was just recently converted to a bed and breakfast and has been featured in some national publications. Rooms are furnished with antiques. Bathrooms are shared at this inn.

Sweet Valley Inn   (419) 746-2750
Division Street
Kelley's Island, Ohio 43438
Handicapped access: steps into house and to bedrooms on second floor

GETTING TO THE ISLAND

In the summertime you can fly or float to the island. But when winter comes, the airplane becomes the islander's link with the mainland for travel, emergencies, and food as there is air service to the islands year-round. During spring, summer, and autumn there are marinas on the island where you can dock your boat. Also, there is ferryboat service hourly from Sandusky and Marblehead.

Griffing Flying Service   (419) 626-5161
Route 6, East
Sandusky, Ohio 44870   Handicapped access: yes

Newman Ferry Service   (419) 626-5557
101 East Shoreline Dr.   Also at Marblehead Dock
Sandusky, Ohio 44870   Handicapped access: yes

20 The Mystique of the Woollybear

YOU CAN USUALLY TELL if a person lives in northern Ohio by whether they know that a woollybear is a caterpillar and not a four-legged bear with a heavy coat.

My colleague at WJW-TV, Dick Goddard, the "Dean" of Ohio weather forecasters, has raised the lowly woollybear caterpillar to near-legendary status. I mean, how many worms do you know that have a festival named after them?

It all started in my living room back in the 1970s. The local elementary school Parent Teachers Association officers were holding a meeting there one evening as I arrived home from work.

"Does anyone have any ideas how we can raise some money?" one of the ladies asked.

"Start a festival named after that woollybear caterpillar that Goddard is always talking about," I said, as I passed through the room.

"If we did," another woman said, "would he make a personal appearance at the festival?"

"Probably," I yelled back from the kitchen. "If you start the festival, I'll ask him."

They did, and Dick did. He not only made a personal appearance; he has been spearheading the festival for nearly a quarter of a century. It is now the largest single-day festival in Ohio, attracting upwards of 150,000 people to watch a two-hour parade through the streets of Vermilion, where the festival is now held. There are also races, games, and woollybear look-alike contests for kids and pets. My personal favorite is the woollybear races. This is where anyone who has a woollybear caterpillar can enter him in a race. It's so exciting. Almost as much fun as watching, say, paint dry, or grass grow.

In all seriousness, the festival has remained true to Dick's original concept. All of the proceeds go to charity. None of the TV or radio personalities, including Dick, make any money from the festival, which has raised thousands of dollars down through the years for local organizations and provided northern Ohio families with a wonderful way to spend an autumn afternoon. The festival is held each year at the end of September or beginning of October, depending on the Cleveland Browns schedule. (Dick is the statistician for the team and so has to schedule the festival when the Browns aren't playing.)

The Woollybear Festival   (216) 967-3467
Vermilion Chamber of Commerce, Liberty Street
Vermilion, Ohio   Handicapped access: yes

GREAT LAKES LORE

One of the attractions in Vermilion year-round is the Great Lakes Historical Society Museum. Here you can find parts of Commodore Oliver Hazard Perry's Flagship, which was sunk in the War of 1812. There is an actual lake freighter wheelhouse, where you can stand and see the lake through the windows. The museum also has an extensive display of artifacts from famous ships that sailed Lake Erie and the other Great Lakes as well.

Great Lakes Historical Society   (216) 967-3467
480 Main Street
Vermilion, Ohio 44089   Handicapped access: yes, but some steps in museum

PIZZA AND OTHER PIES

If you have a pie-lover in your home, then be sure to make a stop at this pie shop in downtown Vermilion. They make pizza pies here that are very good. But their fruit pies are what brings the tourists back time after time. They make deep-dish pies here that are man-sized. Some of the berry pies weigh two pounds or more.

Papa Joe's Pizza and Pies   (216) 967-7330
5590 Liberty Street
Vermilion, Ohio 44089   Handicapped Access: yes

MUSIC BOXES

Another favorite stop for the tour buses in Vermilion is this quaint shop dealing in music boxes from all over the world. They come in all sizes, from antique Reginas to the most modern, computer chip–driven musical boxes.

Musik Box Haus   (216) 967-4744
5551 Liberty Street
Vermilion, Ohio 44089   Handicapped access: yes, but store is very small

OLD SODA FOUNTAIN

There has been an old-fashioned drug store, with a soda fountain, on the corner of Liberty and Main Streets in Vermilion for at least 60 years. Today they no longer make their own syrups and ice cream, but you can still get a wonderful chocolate soda served over the marble counter at the back of the store.

Higgins Pharmacy   (216) 967-4220
Liberty Street
Vermilion, Ohio 44089

A CAPTAIN'S GUEST HOUSE

One of the newest places to spend the night in Vermilion is a Victorian guest house just one block from the lake and two blocks from historic Harbourtown. It has three guest rooms, all with private baths and all air-conditioned. For breakfast, they offer fresh fruit and a sour-cream coffee cake that closely resembles the coffee cake that came from the famous Vermilion bakery, Schwensen's, which, sadly, closed in 1994 after being a Vermilion institution for more than a century.

The guest house offers a large wraparound porch that is a favorite of guests during the summer. The house is located within walking distance of many attractions.

Captain Gilchrist Guest House and Bed and Breakfast   (216) 967-1237
5662 Huron Street
Vermilion, Ohio 44089   Handicapped access: steps to second floor and bedrooms

SOME HOMEMADE CHOCOLATES

There is a new candymaker in town. Bob Brummer is the third generation of his family to make chocolates. His family's candy is well known in New Jersey. Bob married a lady from Vermilion and decided to bring his expertise to Ohio. They offer dozens of flavors of chocolates, all made fresh in the candy kitchen at their store. They will even custom pack a gift box of your favorite chocolates, if you give them some advance notice. They also offer more than 18 varieties of sugar-free candy.

Brummer's Homemade Chocolates   (216) 967-2329
672 Main Street
Vermilion, Ohio 44089   Handicapped access: yes

21 **Camp Perry**

ONE OF MY MEMORIES of growing up during World War II is riding my bicycle to the front gate at Linwood Park, in Vermilion, where we spent our summers, and sitting on an embankment along the edge of U.S. Route 6. I would come there early in the morning to watch a military parade go by. A convoy of Army trucks, led by jeeps with mounted machine guns, passed by Monday through Friday, taking German prisoners from the prisoner of war stockade at Camp Perry in Port Clinton to their jobs in quarries and farms in northern Ohio.

Many of the prisoners were captured during the Normandy invasion of France. They wore U.S. Army fatigues with a large "PW" painted on each pant-leg and across the backs of their shirts. They were mostly very young—men in their teens and twenties, blond-haired and blue-eyed, who appeared to be happy about their situation as prisoners. They would smile and wave to me as they passed. Once in a while one of prisoners would throw me a pack of chewing gum when the jeeps, filled with military policemen, were not too close.

Being only nine years old at the time, I only knew that these men were enemies and I was supposed to hate them. I returned their waves by thumbing my nose at them. However, it was hard to dislike someone who threw gifts and who seemed glad to see you. When they had passed by I scrambled to the edge of the road to collect the packs of gum they had thrown to me. I never told anyone where I got the hard-to-find candy.

It was many years later, when I was serving with the U.S. Marine Corps Reserves and we were spending a weekend at Camp Perry to practice our marksmanship, that I made a connection with those German prisoners of my youth.

We were staying in small tar-paper barracks at the base and, during one evening while lying on my cot, my eyes strayed to some rafters above me. There, scratched in pencil, were German words, a swastika and some dates from 1944. These had been the barracks those German prisoners had lived in. Actually, thousands of Germans, and, earlier, Italians, had been held captive here. In fact, the last two thousand German prisoners were still at Camp Perry in 1946, nearly a year after the war ended, before they were repatriated to Germany.

Today the camp still serves as the home of the National Rifle Matches, the premier shooting event in America, held late each summer at the base.

Camp Perry is now home to the Ohio National Guard and was used in recent years as a training base for reserve forces called up for the Gulf War.

The base is open to the public. There is a small museum at the auditorium commemorating the National Guard unit from Port Clinton that was captured by the Japanese on Bataan in World War II. The post also boasts the largest fishing pier on Lake Erie, which also is open to the public. There is a motel available on the post. Reservations are required.

Camp Perry   (419) 635-4114
U.S. Route 2
Port Clinton, Ohio 43452   Handicapped access: yes

CHARTER FISHING

Some of the best charter-boat fishing on Lake Erie can be found in the Port Clinton area. The downtown dock has a host of charterboats available. The favorite catches here are walleye and Lake Erie perch. There are also "headboats"—boats where you can walk on board with your fishing gear and, for a nominal sum, spend the morning or afternoon fishing with many others in one of the lake's best fishing spots. A charter service we used was:

Shore-Nuf Charters   (419) 734-9999
Drawbridge Marina, 247 Lakeshore Drive
Port Clinton, Ohio 43452   Handicapped access: steps into boat

ELECTRIC TRAINS

In nearby Marblehead, there is a summertime exhibit of electric trains that will warm the heart of any model railroader. A huge room is filled with hundreds of trains in just about every gauge from the tiny N-gauge to the large German style. The exhibit is open from Memorial Day to Labor Day.

Train-O-Rama   (419) 734-5856
6734 East Harbor Road
Marblehead, Ohio   Handicapped access: yes

SMOKED RIBS

This restaurant has offered hickory-smoked ribs, ham, and turkey as its trademark for years, and is also well known for its signature salads. The only drawback is that it closes during the winter months.

The Crow's Nest Restaurant   (419) 734-1742
2170 North Buck Road
Marblehead, Ohio   Handicapped access: yes

A FAST WAY TO THE ISLANDS

A 3,500-horsepower hydrojet catamaran is the fastest ferryboat working Lake Erie. The craft can carry nearly 400 people at a time and makes the run from downtown Port Clinton to Put-in-Bay on South Bass Island in just about 20 minutes. It's a refreshing way to get there, but a word of caution: there are no public bathrooms on board the ship.

The Jet Express   (800) 245-1JET
Put-in-Bay Boat Line Company
Put-in-Bay, Ohio 43456   Handicapped access: yes

22 A Historic Privy

OVER IN NORTHWEST OHIO, in the town of Genoa, they have one of the most unusual structures that has ever been placed on the national register of historic buildings: a privy.

It all started back during the 1976 bicentennial. The local townsfolk wanted to contribute something to the national birthday. They had thought about their town hall, which was nearly 100 years old, but just couldn't stir much excitement about the project because the building was in such bad shape, and it would cost nearly a million dollars to restore its Victorian architecture.

The town faced a crisis. What to do? Then someone suggested the old privy behind the high school. Built in 1865, it was even older than the town hall. The privy was still standing and wouldn't cost much to restore. It was a sturdy brick building that contained no fewer than 12 seats, divided between two rooms with four doors: one for men, one for women, one for boy students, and one for girl students. The privy had fallen on bad times since indoor plumbing became all the rage.

Mrs. Aldo Bergman, of Genoa, led the fight to preserve the privy. She and other volunteers raised all the money and labor needed to restore the building in time for the nation's bicentennial celebration. She admits that all those involved in the project took a lot of ribbing, first from townspeople and then from the national media, when word of their quest for historic recognition for the privy got out. But the federal government took it seriously and granted the little privy national historic status. In fact, Mrs. Bergman says, Congressman Delbert Latta accepted an invitation to be the principal speaker at the dedication ceremony for the outhouse.

And that wasn't the end of the story. Federal officials were so impressed with the efforts of the "save the privy" group, that they gave the community a $750-million-dollar grant to fix up their town hall and list it on the national register of historic buildings, too—which is exactly what the volunteers had wanted to do in the first place.

There is probably a moral to this story, but I am not exactly sure just what it is. However, if you should happen to be in Genoa, be sure to stop and take a look at possibly the only privy in the nation listed, officially, as historic.

A BATHROOM MUSEUM

Also in Northwest Ohio, and related in theme, is perhaps the only museum in Ohio that spells out the history of the bathroom. At Archbold, Ohio, you will find the Sauder Craft Village and Farm. This is a collection of historic buildings from the Northwest Ohio area. At the rear of the village, in a large building, is an eclectic museum that is chock-full of all kinds of equipment and paraphernalia used on early farms. In one corner is an exhibit that traces the history of the bathroom, complete with toilets of every description, bathtubs, and sinks.

The village contains many living history exhibits featuring volunteers, dressed in the costumes of a century ago, still demonstrating crafts such as broom-making, blacksmithing, yarn-spinning, and herb-gardening. There are real farm animals, buggy rides, and barns to wander through. Nearby is a restaurant where fresh country foods are served each day.

If you would like to stay here, check out the newest attraction: the Sauder Heritage Inn, opened in 1994. It is a beautiful, rustic, barn-like inn with large, attractive rooms, each with a private bath. Breakfast is included in the price of a night's lodging.

Sauder Heritage Inn   (419) 446-2541
Sauder Craft Farm and Village, State Route 2
Archbold, Ohio 43502   Handicapped access: yes to both inn and village

SOME BARGAINS ON FURNITURE

Erie Sauder, who founded the Sauder Craft Farm and Village, made his fortune from inexpensive furniture. Many years ago he founded Sauder Furniture, which today is sold across the country in K-Mart, Wal-Mart, and many other department stores. The furniture is mostly office and home items such as desks, entertainment centers, bookcases, and beds, much of it made from particle board and sold unassembled. The main plant is in Archbold and they have a factory outlet here where they dispose of discontinued models, overruns, and some factory seconds—pieces that may have cosmetic blemishes, but be perfect in every other way. You often can find these types of items at a savings here.

Sauder Outlet Store   (419) 446-2711
Lugbill Road and State Route 66
Archbold, Ohio 43502   Handicapped access: yes

A MOST UNUSUAL CAR DEALERSHIP

The sign outside reads "Used Cars for Sale," but this place is more museum than showroom. To be sure, some of the collectible Cadillacs and Peerless automobiles on display are for sale; these are mostly duplicates of other collectible cars this dealer owns. The huge garage has dozens of autos from the early part of this century, all the way up to some of the most modern Cadillacs. The showroom-museum also contains an eclectic collection of signs, bottles, musical instruments, old washing machines, advertising, and many other collectible items. There is an admission charge. They are usually closed on weekends and open only Monday through Friday.

Oberhaus Enterprises, Inc., Cars and Collectibles(419) 446-2773
1488 South Defiance Street (State Route 66, South)
Archbold, Ohio 43502   Handicapped access: yes

CREATIVE ICE CREAM

In far northwest Ohio, Nafziger's Ice Cream is a clear favorite. They have an old-fashioned ice cream parlor at their factory near Archbold, and I liked the creative names they give their flavors, names like "scudbuster" and "moosetracks."

Nafziger's Ice Cream Parlor   (419) 446-2536
22450 County Road "F"
Archbold, Ohio 43502   Handicapped access: yes

LADDERS AND NAKED FURNITURE

Another factory store that is open to the public in this town offers a strange variety of things, from ladders to "naked" furniture (that's furniture with no stain or finish). Like at most factory stores, the best deal here is usually on items being discontinued, or on production overruns.

Archbold Furniture Company Outlet Store   (419) 446-2541
303 East Mechanic Street, P.O. Box 159
Archbold, Ohio 43502

23 A Drive-In for the Dogs

TOLEDO, OHIO MAY HAVE one of the most unique restaurants in the world. Its clientele consists of real animals. In fact, that's all they serve at the Puppy Hut: dogs—and an occasional cat.

The concept was created by Jackie Zajac, who felt sorry for her dogs when they would go to a human drive-in and the animals were largely ignored. The only food available for them was human food, which, usually, was not healthy for the animal.

So Jackie and a partner took over an old photography kiosk in the parking lot of a strip shopping center and opened the first Puppy Hut Drive-In Restaurant. They offer the dogs pet-sized portions of dog biscuits shaped like T-bone steaks, cheeseburgers, and French fries. The homemade biscuits, baked fresh each day by Jackie, contain no salt, sugar, or preservatives. In all, they bake 40 different products for the doggy set.

You can't miss the service people at Puppy Hut; each of them wears a baseball cap with long droopy dog ears hanging off each side.

And be sure to check out the doggy playground at the drive-in. There are park benches for owners to relax on and several concrete fireplugs for the use of the dogs.

The restaurant also sells doggy clothes, leashes, and pet care items.

Some pets (and their owners) have become regulars at the restaurant, stopping almost daily for a pet treat. Jackie Zajac says they have gotten on a first-name basis with many of their pet customers, and when they see the car pull up they already know what the pet likes and have the order ready before the customer reaches the serving window.

The pet restaurant theme has been very successful. The day I visited the Puppy Hut, Jackie spent much of the time answering phone calls inquiring about franchises.

During the cold months, the restaurant is open only on weekends; their schedule is expanded in the spring, summer, and fall.

The Puppy Hut Drive-in   (419) 843-FIDO (419) 478-BARK
5201 Monroe Street
Toledo, Ohio 42623-8436   Handicapped access: yes

THE TOLEDO FIREFIGHTER MUSEUM

A little-used fire station in the city of Toledo has been put to an excellent use. It has become a museum where much of the Toledo department's old equipment is now on display and real, active-duty, firefighters are assigned to the museum to teach fire safety to children and to recall a proud history to visitors.

Firefighter Dave Wernet, who is called "Fireman Dave" by the kids, points out such things as an early lantern from the days when firemen still pulled their pumper to the fire by hand. The youngest member of the department would take the lantern and run ahead of the sweating firemen hauling their pumper down the street screaming at the top of his voice, "FIREMEN COMING! FIREMEN COMING!" He was sort of the predecessor of the siren and red light used today to clear the way for fire trucks.

The museum also offers a look at how firemen lived a hundred years ago. There is the shiny brass pole down which they would slide when answering a fire alarm, and a replica of the stalls that once housed the horses that pulled the giant steam-powered pumper.

Call for hours of operation. Admission is free.

Toledo Firefighter Museum   (419) 478-FIRE
918 Sylvania Avenue
Toledo, Ohio 43623   Handicapped access: yes

A FACTORY STORE

This umbrella factory has been a downtown Toledo landmark for over half a century. You're invited to come right into the factory where they assemble all kinds of umbrellas. While you can't stroll through the aisles, you can see what's happening from the company's store, where they sell some of their discontinued models at a considerable savings. You can also order anything in their catalog.

Haas-Jordan Company   (419) 243-2189
1447 Summit Street
Toledo, Ohio 43623   Handicapped access: steps into plant

OHIO'S ONLY ERIE-FRONT LODGE

Of all the state parks in Ohio, only one offers a lodge with a view of Lake Erie. Maumee Bay State Park is also the newest addition to

Ohio's chain of state-operated parks. The property is located just east of Toledo and includes not only a modern lodge with indoor and outdoor swimming pools and an exercise room but also tennis courts and a state-of-the-art golf course. Futuristic-looking, furnished cabins are also available, sprinkled along the edge of the golf course on the north side of the park. The park is located only minutes from downtown Toledo and is also very close to the Port Clinton-Sandusky Bay area.

Maumee Bay State Park Lodge (800) AT-A-PARK or (419) 836-1466
1750 Maumee Bay Park Road #2
Oregon, Ohio 43618   Handicapped access: yes

CORPORAL KLINGER'S FAVORITE RESTAURANT

Jamie Farr, who portrayed the character Corporal Klinger on the popular TV show M*A*S*H, really did grow up in Toledo, Ohio. The Tony Packo's Restaurant that he used to recall with fondness on the TV show really does exist. In fact, Tony Packo's is a Toledo institution. The walls are covered with—believe it or not—autographed hot dog buns, some of them bearing the names of customers like former President Jimmy Carter and Burt Reynolds! As for the food, spicy Hungarian hot dogs and chili sundaes are a couple of the specialties. The tavern is a very popular spot at lunch and dinner, so be prepared to wait for a seat.

Tony Packo's Cafe   (419) 691-1953
1902 Front Street
Toledo, Ohio 43605   Handicapped access: steps into restaurant

A BASEBALL HALL OF FAME

Ohio's answer to Cooperstown, New York, is located in Toledo. This is the home of the Ohio Baseball Hall of Fame. Tucked away under the stands of the Toledo Mudhen Stadium in Maumee, the museum houses sports memorabilia from all Ohio professional baseball teams, as well as some of the semi-pro teams like the Mudhens. It also includes equipment once owned by Babe Ruth and other legendary stars of baseball. There is an admission fee, and operating times change seasonally. Call for hours.

Ohio Baseball Hall of Fame   (419) 893-9481
Lucas County Recreation Center, 2901 Key Street
Toledo, Ohio 43437   Handicapped access: yes

A TOUR TRAIN

The Toledo area has one of the oldest-running tourist trains in Ohio: the Bluebird has been operating between Waterville and Grand Rapids, Ohio for nearly 20 years. The trip covers a 10-mile stretch along the Maumee River and ends with a dramatic crossing of a long bridge over the river. The operating times change with the seasons. Call for hours.

Bluebird Passenger Train   (419) 878-2177 or (419) 832-4671
The Toledo, Lake Erie and Western Railroad, 49 North Sixth Street
Waterville, Ohio   Handicapped access: steps into train

A GLASS OUTLET STORE

Toledo is the world headquarters of the Libbey Glass Company, and local folks know that a good spot for bargain glassware is the Libbey Company Outlet store at the factory. You can buy their discontinued stock, as well as seconds (cosmetically flawed glassware that can't be sold in stores) at a good savings.

Libbey Glass Factory Outlet Store   (419) 247-5290
1205 Buckeye Street
Toledo, Ohio 43611   Handicapped access: steps into store, narrow aisles

A MUSEUM SHIP

A 600-foot-long lake freighter has become a permanent part of the downtown skyline in Toledo. The ship, which once hauled ore and steel through the Great Lakes, has been retired and turned into a floating museum. Be aware that a lot of walking and climbing are required to see this exhibit.

Museum Ship Willis B. Boyer   (419) 698-8252
Department of Natural Resources, 2201 Ottawa Parkway
Toledo, Ohio 43606

24 Memory Food

DOES THE MENTION OF a fried bologna sandwich stir memories? Do you find yourself back in kindergarten? Well, there is a restaurant in central Ohio that has made fried bologna sandwiches an art form. The G & R Tavern in the small town of Waldo, south of Marion, offers a unique sandwich. It is made of a half-inch slab of homemade bologna that is grilled to a crusty dark brown, covered with a slice of Monterey Jack cheese, topped with a large slice of sweet onion and sweet pickle, then flipped onto a fresh Kaiser roll. To some, it is possibly the closest thing to true ambrosia.

It started back about 32 years ago when the original owners, men named George and Ray, decided to put a fried bologna sandwich on the menu. It wasn't anything unusual. Waldo is farm country and many a young farmer carried fried bologna sandwiches to school each day, especially in the 1930s, '40s, and '50s. Well, George and Roy apparently touched a memory, because their fried bologna sandwich became an instant hit. Their fame spread far from the only downtown street in Waldo. The news reached Columbus, and local newspaper food writers drove up Route 23 to see what all the fuss was about. Soon, food mavens from around the state were stopping in for a fried bologna sandwich. Television personalities from all over also started to get a nostalgic craving for the kindergarten soul food. More stories followed.

Today a sign on the side of their building proclaims the "Best fried bologna sandwich in America." If you challenge that statement, the staff of the G&R will probably whip out a guest book that has comments from across the country, from many who claim to have driven all this distance just to taste their fried bologna sandwich. They can tell you that each week the little country tavern goes through over a half-ton of the specially made bologna. The ingredients are a closely guarded secret that will only be revealed to whoever who buys the tavern. If it is ever sold.

If you visit the G & R, chances are you might find a nun sitting on a bar-stool next to a truck driver, both enjoying a fried bologna sandwich. Also, it is not unusual to see people carrying large grocery bags filled with the sandwiches when they leave.

G & R Tavern   (614) 726-9685
103 North Marion Road (U.S. Route 23)
Waldo, Ohio   Handicapped access: step into building

PRESIDENT WARREN G. HARDING

Although some might say there is a definite correlation between bologna and politics, I choose to think it was just coincidence that a few miles north of Waldo is Marion, Ohio, the home and burial place of the last U.S. president to come from Ohio: Warren G. Harding.

The Harding home is just as he and Mrs. Harding left it in 1920 to go to Washington. President Harding died in office and was brought back to Marion to be buried in a magnificent tomb just a mile or so from his home.

Though Harding's administration was racked with scandal, and many of his appointees went to prison, Harding himself was never charged with wrongdoing. Some historians paint him as a man who relied too much on the advice of political cronies, while others are quick to point out that the good things he accomplished in office have been largely forgotten. One bit of interesting Harding trivia is a speech he gave in 1923 in which he said, "Think more of what you can do for your government than what your government can do for you." Some believe that it was that half-forgotten speech that inspired President John F. Kennedy's more famous line 40 years later.

President Harding Home   (614) 387-9630
380 Mount Vernon Avenue
Marion, Ohio 43302   Handicapped access: steps into house and inside house
Home and small museum at rear of home open for tours, admission charged

A POPCORN MUSEUM

How many towns can claim a museum dedicated to popcorn? Marion, Ohio, can. The Wyandot Popcorn Company is located here, and their collection of popcorn machines and popcorn wagons has finally found a permanent home at the city's new Heritage Hall. The museum also includes a huge stuffed horse, exhibits reflecting other industries that once called Marion home, and a room dedicated to the memory of the town's most famous son, former U.S. President Warren Harding.

Wyandot Popcorn Museum
(614) 387-HALL
Heritage Hall
169 East Church Street
Marion, Ohio 43302
Handicapped access: yes

Wyandot Popcorn Museum

OLD CARS AND A CALLIOPE

The newest attraction in Marion, Ohio, is the private collection of cars owned by local electronics merchant Charley Sens. His passion for cars from the early years of this century has been channeled into a sleek new museum, located behind one of his stores on the edge of town. Dozens of cars can be found here, as well as an airplane and even a calliope. There are lots of benches to rest on while touring the exhibits, and many videotape presentations explaining the history of some of the autos on display. There is a gift shop, and large restrooms to accommodate bus tours. There is an admission fee. Time of operation changes seasonally, so call for hours.

Charley Sens Auto Museum
(614) 389-4686
2074 Marion-Mount Gilead Road, State Route 95, East
Marion, Ohio 43302
Handicapped access: yes

25 Touring with the Governor

I HAVE HAD MANY MEMORABLE trips over the years, but one that particularly sticks in my mind was a dinner by candlelight in a century-old log cabin, tucked away in the hills of southern Ohio. Our hosts were the governor and first lady of Ohio.

It all started when Governor George Voinovich invited my wife, Bonnie, and me to join him, with his wife, Janet, and a group of travel writers from around the United States on a bus tour of some tourist attractions in southern Ohio. The trip was aimed at boosting Ohio tourism by exposing writers to what the Buckeye State had to offer, and showing how important tourism is to Ohio by having the state's chief executive lead the tour.

One of the out-of-state writers later told me that she had accepted the invitation just to see if the governor would really show up to take part in the tour. She said she expected the governor to just drop in sometime over the weekend, give a speech to the writers and then depart, leaving his underlings to lead the tour. The writer joined the tour just as the bus was leaving. When we arrived at our first destination, she asked when the governor was going to arrive and was shocked to learn that the nice couple she had been chatting with on the bus—the ones wearing sweatshirts and walking shoes, who had just introduced themselves as George and Janet—were the governor and first lady.

In fact, the governor and Mrs. Voinovich didn't exactly lead the tour. They just joined the rest of us in wandering in and out of attractions, asking as many questions as the writers did of the people in charge at each destination.

The first evening ended at the Inn at Cedar Falls, a hundred-plus-year-old log cabin and complex located in the heart of the Hocking Hills State Park. It was a beautiful Ohio autumn night and candles glowed in each of the cabin's windows. Inside, innkeeper Ellen Grinsfelder and her staff had been working to prepare a gourmet feast for the writers and the governor and his staff. During dinner, the governor and Mrs. Voinovich table-hopped, talking with all of the writers, and reminiscing about their affection for the Hocking Hills area. The governor said he had first discovered it when he was a student at nearby Ohio University. Janet Voinovich remembered the times when their children were small and the whole Voinovich family would rent a cabin for a vacation in the area.

Our accommodations for the night were in a converted barn located behind the cabin. Each of the rooms, while rustic, had a bathroom and electricity—but no TV, no radio, and no clock! As the dinner ended, we wandered up the path to our rooms, the path illuminated only by moonlight.

In the morning we were fed a wonderful gourmet breakfast and had time to wander the gardens around the cabin where many of the herbs and vegetables for the dining room are grown.

The inn sits in the middle of the 10,000-acre Hocking Hills State Park. It is only minutes away from some of Ohio's most famous attractions, like Old Man's Cave and Ash Cave, with miles of trails to hike and wonderful rock formations to see. While autumn is spectacular here, each season lends a special beauty to the park system.

Inn At Cedar Falls   (614) 385-7489
21190 State Route 374
Logan, Ohio 43138 Handicapped access: steps into cabin and sleeping quarters

Hocking Hills State Parks   (614) 385-6165 or (614) 385-6841
20160 State Route 664 South
Logan, Ohio 43138   Handicapped access: yes

A STEAM TRAIN RIDE

One of Ohio's first steam excursion trains is located in nearby Nelsonville. The railroad, operated by volunteers, uses both steam- and diesel-powered engines to give tourists a slow ride through the Hocking Valley. Tickets can be obtained at the depot in Nelsonville. The train usually runs seasonally, but does make special runs on holidays. Call for schedule.

Hocking Valley Scenic Railroad   (614) 335-0382
P.O. Box 427
Nelsonville, Ohio 45764

BARGAIN BOOTS

You can buy some boots at bargain prices and take a tour of the boot factory in Nelsonville. This is where the famous Rocky boots are made. The factory outlet store sells seconds and overruns at a considerable savings. Tours are available when the plant is in operation. The outlet store is open Monday through Saturday.

Brooks Shoe Company   (614) 753-3130
Canal Street
Nelsonville, Ohio 45764   Handicapped access: steps in plant

COLLEGE FOR HOTEL MANAGERS

There is a most unusual motel in this town. The Hocking Technical College operates the facility as a training ground for its students in hotel management, restaurant management, and several other related fields. The motel is staffed by advanced students and supervised by instructors. Often the service and food is superb, but you have to keep in mind that this is a training facility. Overall it is an inexpensive place to stay and eat while visiting the area.

Quality Inn, Hocking   (800) 221-2222 or (614) 753-3531
State Route 691
Nelsonville, Ohio 45764   Handicapped access: yes

From My Mailbag...

Neil Zurcher

My friends and I took your advice and went to an Amish restaurant. We were looking forward to what you described as "real Amish food." We were very disappointed when the waitress brought us fried chicken, roast beef, and mashed potatoes and gravy. We can have this at home. We were expecting real ethnic food. What a disappointment.!!

--Unhappy in Euclid

26 The Forgotten Governor

JOHN BROWN OF MEDINA SERVED as lieutenant governor of Ohio longer, and under more governors, than any other Lieutenant governor in the state's history. He wanted to be governor of Ohio and unsuccessfully ran for the office at least once. He was never elected to the top office, but through an unusual chain of events he finally succeeded in becoming the state's chief executive—if only for 11 days.

Back in 1957, when Governor Frank Lausche succeeded in his attempt to win a U.S. Senate seat, he resigned as Governor 11 days before his term ended. Lausche wanted to be sworn in early in Washington to gain a few days' seniority over other freshman senators. Under Ohio's laws of succession, John Brown became the Governor for those last 11 days of Lausche's term.

Now no one expected Brown to do much more than just be a caretaker and sort of keep the Governor's office running until fellow Republican, C. William O'Neil, who had been elected to succeed Lausche as governor, took office 11 days later.

Brown decided if he was going to be governor in name, he would also be governor in fact. He and his wife immediately moved into the governor's mansion on East Broad Street. They held a reception and invited any Ohioan who wanted to see where the chief executive lived.

He addressed the state legislature, pleading for additional school funding, and calling their attention to the problems resulting from the rising urbanization of rural areas. He also called for conservation of Ohio's natural resources.

In his 11 days in office, he also called two sides together in a troublesome telephone strike in southern Ohio and was instrumental in hammering out a settlement.

Perhaps the most controversial thing he did as governor was to commute the first degree murder convictions of four prison inmates to second degree murder, making them eligible for parole.

When his 11 days were over, he quietly moved out of the governor's mansion and returned to his hometown of Medina. In later years he would again and again be elected to the office of lieutenant governor, but never to the top job. Nevertheless, during 11 days in 1957, John W. Brown of Medina truly was the Governor of Ohio.

THE STATE CAPITOL

There are 10 acres in the center of Columbus, at the intersection of Broad and High streets, where the business of Ohio is conducted. The State House, some critics say, looks like a wheel of cheese on a box. Others point to the Greek Doric structure with pride and claim it is unique among America's state capitol buildings.

It contains the state house of representatives, the state senate, the state supreme court, and the offices of various top state leaders, including the governor.

The rotunda is open for tours seven days a week. Tours of legislative chambers and other offices in the building can be arranged Monday through Friday. At the time of this writing, the State House is undergoing extensive renovation and is not expected to be completed until 1996. Some areas that are completed are open for tours.

The State House   (614) 466-2125
Broad & High Street
Columbus, Ohio 43215   Handicapped access: yes

COSI

It stands for Center Of Science and Industry. It is really a hands-on, fun place for the entire family.

There is always something new at COSI, from its replica of a working coal mine in the basement, to the kids' room on the second floor—where they can have water fights and not get wet—to the steel beam in front of the building, where anyone brave enough to do it can ride a bicycle across the beam, 20 feet off the ground, in relative safety to prove the theory of balance. The good news here is that COSI will soon be moving to new and larger quarters just across the Scioto River in downtown Columbus. That means more wonderful and exciting things to do for kids and adults alike.

COSI   (614) 228-2674
280 East Broad Street
Columbus, Ohio 43215   Handicapped access: yes

SLATE RUN FARM

I have long said that Ohio's greatest treasures are the metropark districts that abound in the state. These local parks get very little statewide publicity and many are almost unknown, yet they offer everything from caves to wonderful state-of-the-art nature exhibits, vistas, canyons, and a host of things to do for the entire family.

In Columbus, the Metropolitan Park District operates the Slate Run Farm, located in nearby Pickaway County. The farm is frozen in time. It is just like it was at the turn of the twentieth century. Horses are still used to till the earth. The farmhouse still uses wood cookstoves. The workers here are all in period costumes and, when questioned, react as though the century were just starting. Kids are allowed to help with chores, like gathering eggs and cultivating the garden by hand, or use an old rope swing under a tree beside the farmhouse.

Slate Run Farm   (614) 891-0700
For directions contact:
Metropolitan Park District of Columbus, P.O. Box 29169
Columbus, Ohio 43229   Handicapped access: yes, but steps into some buildings

THE SANTA MARIA

A replica of Christopher Columbus's flagship, the Santa Maria, is docked in downtown Columbus in the Scioto River.

The wooden ship is as close to being a copy of the original vessel as possible. Volunteers wear costumes of the period and act out the roles of members of Columbus's crew when visitors are aboard. The ship is open different hours in different seasons, so it is a good idea to call for the operating schedule.

Columbus Santa Maria, Inc.   (614) 460-3725
770 Twin Rivers Drive
Columbus, Ohio 43216   Handicapped access: steps on ship

A REALLY BIG BURGER

German Village in downtown Columbus is an example of what can be done with a deteriorating neighborhood. Private capital, over the years, has restored much of this ethnic community from a slum to an attractive residential neighborhood and popular dining area. One of my favorite spots is an old tavern that serves one of the largest hamburgers in Columbus. Called a "Thurmanburger," it contains nearly one pound of ground meat, cheese, ham, and other condiments. It's more than a meal, all by itself.

Thurman Cafe   (614) 443-1570
183 Thurman Avenue
Columbus, Ohio 43212Handicapped access: narrow aisles, crowded dining area

CATALOG BARGAINS

Have you have ever wondered what happens to that merchandise you sent back to J.C. Penney's Catalog Service? It ends up in a giant outlet store in Columbus.

The store is located right next to the catalogue distribution center, and returned merchandise, along with discontinued items, is offered for sale. The merchandise is constantly changing, so there is always something new. A careful shopper can save up to 50 percent on some items.

J.C. Penney Outlet Store   (614) 868-0250
2361 Park Crescent Road
Columbus, Ohio 43232   Handicapped access: yes

A MOTORCYLE MUSEUM

Perhaps one of the more unusual museums in the state is located in the Columbus suburb of Westerville. It contains the history of motorcycles, from the earliest models, which were made on wooden frames, to the most modern types from the world over.

Motorcyle Museum   (614) 868-0250
33 Collegeview
Westerville, Ohio 43081   Handicapped access: yes.

AN UNUSUAL SHOPPING MALL

One of the most unusual shopping malls in Ohio is located on the north side of Columbus. It is designed to make you feel that you are walking down the street of a small French village. There are cobblestones and quaint bridges, little shops with balcony apartments hanging overhead. At the end of the street is a giant statue of a French soldier in a World War I uniform. The shopping center contains many small shops, restaurants and theaters, as well as a large food court with foods from many nationalities.

The Continent Shopping Center   (614) 764-3327
6076 Busch Boulevard
Columbus, Ohio 43229   Handicapped access: yes

A HISTORY OF FLIGHT

Tucked away in a corner near the Columbus Airport is a small museum that portrays Ohio's role in the history of commercial aviation. Although small, the exhibits are well displayed and very interesting. For example, they have the world's only inflatable airplane (made by Goodyear), which was designed to be dropped to downed aviators to help them rescue themselves.

Ohio History of Flight Museum   (614) 231-1300
4275 Sawyer Road
Columbus, Ohio 43212   Handicapped access: yes

A HAMBURGER MUSEUM

The original Wendy's Old Fashioned Hamburger Restaurant is still standing and, in fact, is still serving Wendy's Hamburgers. Now it has also been turned into the official Wendy's Museum. Featuring memorabilia like the first homemade dress worn by Wendy Thomas, (for whom the hamburger chain is named) and even the first skillet that founder Dave Thomas used to sample hamburger that he was buying for his restaurant. For laughs, they have a video machine that shows some of the out-takes of Dave Thomas's Wendy's commercials. Admission to the museum is free. You can see it while you are eating lunch—at Wendy's, of course.

Wendy's Museum
Wendy's Old Fashioned Hamburgers
257 East Broad Street
Columbus, Ohio
or for information, write to:

Wendy's International   (614) 764-3327
4288 West Dublin-Granville Road
Dublin, Ohio 43017   Handicapped access: yes

THE LAST WHISTLE

A Columbus firm holds the distinction of being the last American manufacturer of whistles—the kind policemen, referees, and band directors use. They make the 24-karat-gold-plated presentation whistles that are given each year to the officials in the Superbowl game. They call this model "The most expensive whistle made." It sells for about $50. By the way, these presentation whistles are available to the public. They make a nice gift if you have a friend or relative that uses a whistle.

The factory is open for tours during working hours, but reservations are required.

American Whistle Corporation   (800) 876-2918 or (614) 846-2918
6540 Huntley Road
Columbus, Ohio 43229   Handicapped access: yes

From My Mailbag...

Dear Neel Zurker,

Why do you drive a Tank??? Why can'T you drive a car like everybody else??

--Perplexed

27 'Tis the Season

AFTER ALL THE HOLIDAY STORIES I have done down through the years, I still believe that one of the best places to give yourself a holiday boost is in the restored canal town of Roscoe Village in Coshocton.

They begin the season with an outdoor candle-lighting ceremony about the first weekend in December. A well-known person is usually invited to be the "official candle lighter." I had been invited and arrived on a very cold and dark December night. The town looked like a page from some Dickens novel, with frost painting the edges of windows. Guides from the various attractions in the village were all dressed in 19th-century frock coats or hoop skirts. Streetlights from another era illuminated the walks and roadways, where thousands of people milled about waiting for the ceremony to begin.

A stage had been placed halfway down the main street, Whitewoman Street. Beside the street, on one side, was a steep hillside that led upwards to the next street. On the other side were the stores that had serviced canal boats and their crews a hundred years before.

A brass ensemble was wandering the streets playing Christmas carols, while small groups of carolers strolled in front of the stores singing the songs of the season.

My duties were simple. I was given a brief introduction, to polite applause, and as I stepped forward to the podium, the lights along the streets went out. I struck a match and lit a candle I was holding. For a moment, as I wished the crowd a Merry Christmas, I held in my hand the only light on the street. In the darkness several thousand people stood crowded around the stage.

I walked across the stage and, leaning towards the crowd, started to light other candles held by the crowd. The light spread outward from my candle and, in moments, pinpoints of light had climbed the hill behind me and ignited a river of candles in the street on both sides of me. I led the crowd in the song "Silent Night." Never before had the song seemed so real, so personal as it did this magical night in Roscoe Village as I stood bathed in the light of thousands of candles.

Restored canal town Roscoe Village is open year-round to tourists. Many of the shops and stores have been recreated as living history museums, where you can watch long-ago crafts still being practiced by experts. There are also antique stores, and a host of places to eat and buy souvenirs and the crafts created in the village. For more information contact:

Roscoe Village Foundation   (614) 622-9310
381 Hill Street
Coshocton, Ohio 43812   Handicapped access: yes

RIDE A REAL CANAL BOAT

The Monticello II is a concrete version of the boats that once traversed Ohio canals. Today, instead of hauling freight, it carries tourists on hourly runs over a mile-long stretch of the old canal. The boat is pulled by a pair of workhorses and follows the same towpath that was used over a century ago. The canal boat ride is only available during the summer months.

Monticello II Canal Boat Ride   (614) 622-9310
Lake Park
Coshocton, Ohio 43812   Handicapped access: steps into boat

FOLK MUSIC INSTRUMENTS

Early music instruments used by pioneers and canal workers can still be purchased here, including hammer dulcimers (or mountain dulcimers), banjos, and guitars. This small music store near the edge of the canal offers quality instruments and music.

Wildwood Music   (614) 622-4224
Roscoe Village
Coshocton, Ohio 43812   Handicapped access: steps into building

WHERE TO STAY

One of the nicest places to stay in the village is the recently constructed Roscoe Village Inn. Built to blend in with its historic surroundings, it appears to be centuries old yet contains all the modern amenities, like private baths, televisions, and restaurants. There are also several bed and breakfast establishments in the village.

Roscoe Village Inn   (614) 622-9310
Whitewoman Street
Coshocton, Ohio 43812   Handicapped access: yes

OHIO'S ONLY FLAG FACTORY

The only American Flag factory in Ohio is located here. Millions of editions of "Old Glory" are manufactured each year. Sadly, tours of the plant have been discontinued because of the sheer numbers of tourists who wanted to go through the plant. The factory still has a gift shop open to the public where you can buy all sizes of American flags for your home, auto, or boat.

Colonial Flag Company   (614) 622-4447
14th Street, P.O. Box 507
Coshocton, Ohio 43812   Handicapped access: steps into shop

ANTIQUE MALL

One of the first antique malls in Ohio was opened in this old Victorian home in a lovely residential section of downtown Coshocton. One of the nice features is a library where you can look up any antique they have for sale.

Coshocton Antique Center   (614) 622-3223
309 South Fourth Street
Coshocton, Ohio 43812   Handicapped access: steps into building

One Tank Tip #8
Eating on the Road

Carry a small cooler with drinks and snacks in it on long road trips. This saves money, lets you have an impromptu picnic along the road, and provides emergency food when it's late and you don't feel like looking for a restaurant.

28 The Fastest-Growing Tourist Area in Ohio

THE LARGEST AMISH POPULATION in the world is not in Lancaster, Pennsylvania; it is in Ohio in the Wayne-Holmes-Tuscarawas County area. These plain people, who reject cars for horses and buggies, and electric lights for kerosene lamps, draw millions of tourists to Ohio each year.

Amish cottage industries are now being joined by other entrepreneurs who are springing up like Amish flower gardens throughout the region. New inns and bed and breakfasts are being added almost daily. Restaurants that reflect the Amish "meat and potatoes" cuisine also are appearing at nearly every crossroads. Cheese factories that once relied almost totally on supermarket sales around the state are enlarging their facilities and opening new showrooms, selling their product to tourists so fast that it hardly has time to age. Tour buses wander quiet back roads, leaving plumes of dust behind them as they search out quilt shops and home bakeries. Portions of State Route 39 have been enlarged to four lanes to handle the increased traffic that sometimes creates big-city traffic jams in crossroads villages in the region.

If you are going to be visiting this busy tourist area, here are some things to remember to make your trip more pleasurable.

Don't visit on a Sunday. You will find almost everything closed. The Amish are very religious and do not believe in working on the Sabbath. Many non-Amish merchants, who respect the Amish beliefs, also are closed. If you do plan a Sunday trip be sure to call ahead to the attractions you want to visit to be sure they are open.

Try to slate your trip for the middle of the week. Weekends are very busy and roads are crowded, as are shops, stores, and restaurants. Even during weekdays, plan on standing in line at many of the more popular restaurants. The very best time to visit Amish country is in the off-season, November through April, on a rainy day, in the middle of the week. You often have the stores and attractions to yourself. Also it's a time when there are price savings at many of the inns and bed and breakfast establishments.

When dealing with the Amish, leave your camera in the car. The Amish do not like to have their pictures taken; it violates their religious beliefs. If you must take a picture, ask their permission first, don't just stick the camera in their faces and fire away.

Take a cooler or ice chest with you, especially in hot weather, to take advantage of the many good fresh foods that are for sale in Amish country, like cheese, homemade pies, bread, fresh bacon, and hams. If you forget your cooler, try to schedule your trip so that the place where you are picking up the food items is the last stop before you start home.

Wear comfortable clothes and be prepared for your car to get very dirty. Many of the roads are gravel and dirt, and there is always dust and mud to contend with. Also, be especially careful and courteous on the roadways. Many blind hills suddenly reveal a slow-moving Amish buggy on the other side. And be patient when trapped behind a buggy. Remember that the horse might be frightened by a blast from your automobile horn.

If you plan to spend the night and like to end your day with an alcoholic beverage, be sure to bring it with you, because most of the Amish area is "dry." There are few bars in the small villages, and most of the inns and bed and breakfasts do not offer alcoholic beverages. There are exceptions in Millersburg and in Sugarcreek and some of the larger towns.

Also, you will find that most restaurants and bed and breakfasts do not allow smoking inside.

Many of the Amish businesses and restaurants and attractions do accept major credit cards

A good place to start your trip through the Amish land of Ohio is near the town of Berlin at the Mennonite Information Center. Here you can see a cyclorama, or large circular painting, of the history of the Amish and Mennonite people. The work, which is 10 feet tall and 265 feet long, took 14 years to complete. The artist, Heinz Gaugel, is presently working on other paintings in the center. Knowledgeable guides will answer questions about the faith and customs of the area. There is a craft and souvenir shop in the building as well as some large, clean public rest rooms. Admission is charged to see the cyclorama.

Mennonite Information Center   (216) 893-3192
P.O. Box 324, 5798 County Road 77   Admission charge for cyclorama
Berlin, Ohio 44610   Handicapped access: yes

THE AMISH WAY OF LIFE

A close-up look at the Amish lifestyle can be had at an authentic Amish farm, open to the public, just outside of Berlin. The farm consists of a main house, the grandparents' house, barns, and a group of craft shops that have been opened by the present owner. There are also Amish buggy rides available.

The Amish Farm   (216) 893-2951
P.O. Box 61, State Route 39, East   Admission charged
Berlin, Ohio 44610   Handicapped access: gravel driveways and steps into some buildings

THE FIRST CHEESE FACTORY

The area's cheese production began in the early 1930s with the opening of Heini's Bunker Hill Cheese Company, the first really large maker of Swiss cheese in the area. Today, the Dauwalder family still operates the business which now ships cheese all over the world. They offer free tours of the cheese-making operation during the morning hours on weekdays, and have a salesroom where you can have free samples from the more than 50 varieties of cheese that they make and sell here—everything from Swiss to chocolate cheese. That's right, chocolate. It tastes a little like fudge. Heini's also offers a series of shops in its complex that sell fudge, crafts, souvenirs, fresh baked goods, and many other things.

Heini's Bunker Hill Cheese Company   PH:(216) 893-2131 or FAX (216) 893-2027
6005 County Road 77
Berlin, Ohio 44654   Handicapped access: yes

A ROMANTIC HIDEAWAY

In Berlin, tucked away on a back street within walking distance of the main street, is a quaint bed and breakfast that offers a unique hideaway for honeymoons, anniversary celebrations, or any special occasion. There are two rooms in the main house and two small cottages that were once carriage barns. The cottages offer cathedral ceilings, floor-to-ceiling fireplaces, four-poster beds with Amish quilts, a whirlpool bath for two with lights, and even a small waterfall! In the morning, the owner discreetly places a tray with a large breakfast on it on a cart outside the door. Reservations are an absolute must here almost anytime.

Donna's Country Bed and Breakfast   (216) 893-3068
East Street, P.O. Box 307
Berlin, Ohio 44610   Handicapped access: yes

TOUR A FORGE

This is the newest attraction in the Amish area. This Pennsylvania-based company has opened a barn-like gift shop and forge on the outskirts of Berlin. They make hammered aluminum and copper plates, trays, dishes, and other metal products. The forge, where the craftsmen do their work, is in the rear of the building and is open for tours. There is also a small museum in the building with hammered aluminum products from the past and also the world's largest Amish buggy.

Tour groups are welcome.

Wendell August Forge   (800) 923-4438
U.S. Route 62
Berlin, Ohio 44610   Handicapped access: yes

A NICE MOTEL

Most of the motels and inns in this area are sparkling clean and many offer wonderful pastoral views of the Amish countryside. On the outskirts of Berlin there is a small family-run motel that has been in business since before the tourist rush began. It sits on a hillside overlooking some Amish farms below. The rooms are large and offer cable TV, good-sized bathrooms, and comfortable beds. At the height of the tourist season reservations are usually required, and they are a good idea any time of year.

Berlin Village Inn   (216) 893-2861
State Route 39, West
Berlin, Ohio, 44654   Handicapped access: yes

A POOL, A RESTAURANT, A MOTEL

While you don't find many places to stay in Amish country that offer big city amenities like swimming pools and exercise rooms, there are exceptions. On the outskirts of Berlin, operated by the same folks who run the Amish Farm, is a motel-restaurant complex that measures up to those in many big cities. The motel, in one building, is built on the edge of a farmer's meadow where you can usually find cows and horses grazing. Each of the rooms has a small balcony, cable TV, and a large bathroom and bedroom. Next door is the restaurant, with a glass wall that overlooks the pasture. A fireplace dominates the main portion of the dining room. The specialty is Amish-style cooking with fresh baked goods. On the other side of the motel is a fitness center that is open to motel guests. It includes exercise equipment, a spa and swimming pool, and a health bar.

The Amish Country Inn & Dutch Harvest Restaurant   (216) 893-3000
State Route 39 West
Berlin, Ohio 44654   Handicapped access: yes

A WAY TO TAKE AMISH COUNTRY HOME WITH YOU

If you would like some beautiful photos of the Amish and their countryside, watch for the work of local resident Doyle Yoder in the gift stores, craft shops, and restaurants in the area. Doyle was born and raised with the Amish. Their trust of him is apparent in the sensitive photos that he takes in every season of the year. He has also collaborated in a large photo book that shows the Amish communities across the United States. It, too, is available in most shops in the region. For a catalogue of Doyle's work and other books and pictures he offers, write to:

Doyle Yoder, Photographer
Amish Country Calendar, P.O. Box 424
Berlin, Ohio 44610

From My Mailbag...

Dear Mr. Zurcher,

You forgot to mention on your show about Columbus that they offer tours of the Anheuser-Busch Beer Company. You must have Anheuser's disease.

--Disturbed in Wooster

29 **The Amish Capital**

MILLERSBURG, OHIO COULD EASILY be called the capital of the Amish region. It is the county seat of Holmes County, where the vast majority of the world's Amish live. In fact the county courthouse has a hitching rail for Amish horses on a street out front.

They also once had parking meters for the horses, just like they did on other streets for automobiles. Sadly, the parking meters, which used to make such a wonderful photographic opportunity for tourists, are now gone and I believe it is my fault.

Some years ago I noticed that while police were ticketing overtime parked automobiles, I did not see any tickets on the Amish buggies that were also parked at expired meters.

I went to see Millersburg Chief of Police Darryl Weiss and asked him why it was that while motorists seemed to be getting tickets, the Amish were not.

"That's not so," he said. "We ticket the Amish, the problem is tracking down just who the horse and buggy belongs to."

He went on to point out an obvious fact I had missed. The Amish are not required to license their buggies, or horses for that matter, like motorists are. So when a police officer goes to write a parking ticket for an overdue meter and the culprit is a dark horse and a black buggy, how does he identify it? Especially if five other practically identical horses and buggies are parked legally right beside it!

I granted that the chief had a problem.

"How do you handle the situation?" I asked.

"We usually just write the ticket and leave the license number and make of car section blank or write "horse" where it says "car," he said. "Then we hope they will come in, or send in the fine."

"Do they?" I asked.

Chief Weiss paused.

"Sometimes they do, sometimes they don't," he finally answered. "I guess it's really not fair to other motorists and we ought to do something about it."

A couple of months later the parking meters were gone all over the downtown.

Was it because of my inquiry, or was it just the village fathers reacting to the arrival of a large discount store on the outskirts of town with an effort to keep local customers downtown?

I guess I'll never know, but I sort of miss the sight of the horses tied to the parking meters at the courthouse.

SPIRITS AND TRADITION

You can find both at the Hotel Millersburg, built more than a century and a half ago. It has recently been modernized and is one of the few places in Holmes County where you can have an alcoholic drink with your dinner.

The governor of Ohio has stayed here, as well as other celebrities.

The rooms offer cable TV, large modern bathrooms, and the convenience of being in downtown Millersburg. The owner also has a farm and, if you ask, will probably lend you a bamboo fishing pole and give you directions to the farm. They're friendly folks around here.

Hotel Millersburg   (216) 674-1457
9 West Jackson Street
Millersburg, Ohio 44654   Handicapped access: steps to second floor

A REALLY BIG ICE-CREAM CONE

If you like ice cream, I mean lots of ice cream, we have a store for you. It's a small grocery store in downtown Millersburg where they don't sell ice-cream cones by the dip. They sell them by the pound! A "double" contains nearly a pound of ice cream, and that's a really big ice-cream cone.

The Grocery Bag   (216) 674-0833
106 North Clay Street
Millersburg, Ohio 44654   Handicapped access: yes

AN INTRODUCTION TO THE COUNTY

A publication gives maps, recipes, and stories of the Amish area, as well as some beautiful photographs. If you plan to spend any time in the area or just enjoy country stories and photos, you might want to subscribe to it. It's published by a local couple, Fran and Abe Mast, who grew up in the area and know just about everybody.

The Holmes County Traveler Magazine   (216) 674-2300
P.O. Box 358, County Road 623
Millersburg, Ohio 44654

SHOPPING MADE EASY

An old grocery store in Millersburg has been turned into a shopper's paradise. More than a hundred craftspeople now call it home. They each rent a small booth, and the store management looks after their merchandise and sells it for them. You can find Amish crafts, like quilts, paintings, woodwork, and a multitude of other items alongside watercolors, jewelry, brooms, and cement lawn figures. Just name it; they probably have it. This store is open seven days a week. However, Amish booths are closed on Sundays in respect of Amish customs.

They also recently opened a restaurant buffet that serves Amish-style food.

Millersburg Gallery of Crafts   (216) 674-5300
75 East Clinton Street
Millersburg, Ohio 44654   Handicapped access: yes

A FIREPLACE IN THE BEDROOM

If you are looking for a more private place to spend the night here, try a bed and breakfast. In Millersburg, a former Victorian home that once belonged to the local doctor has been converted into a bed and breakfast and a tea room. One of the bedrooms has its own fireplace and private bath and is beautifully furnished. The tea room is open for light lunches, teas, and special occasions by reservation.

Bigham House of Millersburg Bed and Breakfast   (216) 674-BEDS or 674-2337
154 South Washington Street
Millersburg, Ohio 44654   Handicapped access: steps into house and to second floor

WATCH IT MADE RIGHT BEFORE YOUR EYES

This woolen mill on the outskirts of Millersburg has been here for over a century, and the same family has operated it nearly that long.

You are invited to drop in any day they are in operation and watch wool being turned into rich colorful rugs. They also have a store where they sell wool clothing and other wood products.

Rastetter's Woolen Mill   (216) 674-2103
5802 State Route 39
Millersburg, Ohio 44654   Handicapped access: narrow aisles in shop

A DIFFERENT KIND OF PLACE TO STAY

The Inn at Honey Run is not your ordinary Amish Country inn. To be sure, it has Amish help and it is located far off the main road in the center of Amish farm land, but the similarities end there. Owner Marge Stock, formerly of Cleveland, has built a hideaway that attracts the likes of the governor and his wife when they are trying to escape the pressures of public life.

The Inn itself cannot be seen from the highway. It is hidden among tall trees. The menu reflects the area, but also includes farm-raised trout, steaks, and other country delicacies prepared in original recipes. Usually there is a need for reservations for both lunch and dinner at the Inn.

As for the sleeping accommodations, they too are original. Several sleeping units have been built into the side of a hill (and look like a giant beehive from below). There are beautifully fitted guest houses on top of the hill, nestled in groves of trees, each with fireplace, kitchen, bedrooms, and all modern amenities. The inn is truly an out-of-the-ordinary place to spend a night or a weekend in Amish country.

The Inn At Honey Run　　　　(216) 674-0011
6920 County Road 203
Millersburg, Ohio 44654　　　　Handicapped access: yes

AN OLD-FASHIONED MEN'S STORE

This store has been in the same family, selling the same thing—men's clothing—since before the Civil War. It has also been in the same location all those years, surviving wartime shortages, depressions, changing lifestyles, and even the competition of giant discount stores.

The secret, says the store's owner, is they still give old-fashioned service—like keeping a man's sizes on record for future use by the customer or his relatives who want to buy gifts. Alteration service, done by a fine seamstress to make sure every suit fits, and even overnight drycleaning are available.

Maxwell's Men's Store　　　　(216) 674-4936
Jackson Street at the square
Millersburg, Ohio 44654　　　　Handicapped access: yes

EAT WITH THE AMISH

If you would like to have a meal with an Amish family, then you will have to write to them because they have no telephone. The last time we checked, this family opens their home to small groups by reservation and cooks them a typical Amish feast with roast beef, turkey, ham, and all the trimmings, depending on how much you want to spend. It's a pleasant way to learn more about the Amish and enjoy a good meal at the same time. Just write to:

Andy and Maude Raber   no phone, they will mail directions
Raber's Home Cooking, Route 4, Box 183
Millersburg, Ohio 44654
Handicapped access: tell them your needs in your letter; they will advise

---

One Tank Tip #9
Try a Bed and Breakfast

If motels are full and you didn't make reservations, ask the clerk for a list of local bed and breakfasts. Often they have vacancies when motels near main roads are full.

30 Back Roads Of Ohio's Amish Land

IT WAS A FOGGY SPRING MORNING. It had rained almost all night, and now the mist of morning was just starting to burn away as the sun teased us with the promise of a balmy day.

Videographer Bill West and I had driven to this gravel road in the Doughty Valley, east of Millersburg, to do a report on what I called an "Amish motel": a collection of log cabins on a hillside operated as a campground by an Amish family. The cabins had just been completed a few weeks earlier, and we had convinced the publicity-shy Amish owners that it would be good for their business if we showed their new enterprise. We had also promised not to take any pictures of the owners.

The cabins were scattered down a hillside that overlooked the Doughty Creek, which flows through the valley. Across the valley, you could make out the stainless steel storage tanks at the Guggisberg Cheese Company, just now emerging from the morning fog.

I stepped out of our car and immediately noticed a strong odor of horse manure. But being in Amish Country, where horses are the main means of transportation, I gave it little thought. Bill was setting up his camera as I walked to the edge of the hillside to get a good look at the cabins. The wet ground seemed to be covered with straw. I stepped onto the steep path that headed towards the cabins and I felt my feet start to slip. I threw up my arms to regain my balance, but then both feet went out from underneath me and I landed on my back and started to slide, through the mud and straw, down the hill.

When I finally came to a stop about 30 feet down the hillside, I realized where the smell of horse manure had been coming from. They had just seeded the hillside and spread fresh manure on it for fertilizer. I was now coated from the top of my head to the bottom of my heels with a mixture of horse dung, straw, and wet mud.

Videographer West and an Amish woman came skidding down the hill to help. They helped me to my feet, both trying—not too successfully—to smother their laughter as I stood up, mud and dung dripping from my hair, my back, and my legs.

"Where's the bathroom?" I asked the Amish lady.

She covered her mouth with one hand to disguise a smile and

used the other to point to a small wooden building at the bottom of the hill.

"There it is," she said, "but there's no running water here."

"Where's the nearest place I can clean myself up?" I asked.

She pointed across the valley towards the Guggisberg Cheese Company's store.

I started walking up the hill towards our newscruiser. As I approached the door, Bill West jumped in front of me and said. "Where are you going?"

I explained I was going to get in the car and have him drive me down to the cheese company so I could use their modern bathroom.

"You're not going to get in my newscruiser like that!" he said, refusing to budge.

"Well, how am I supposed to get over there then?" I replied in a testy voice.

He pointed to the hood of his car.

A few minutes later, clinging to the hood of the newscruiser, spread-eagled across the car like some large animal bagged in a hunt, I was driven down the hill and across the valley, past startled Amish families in their buggies, to the cheese factory, where I was finally able to wash up.

As to how you rent those cabins, most of the Amish don't have telephones. But if you call on a Monday morning, they station one of the Amish youngsters at a pay telephone across the street from the cabins to take messages about reservations. Just let it ring a long time, in case he has decided to wander down the road to explore the ditch.

Actually, the cabins, while primitive, are quite nice. They offer a wood-burning stove, kerosene lamps, all the cookware and bedding for a family of at least four, and furniture for a very reasonable price. And, at the top of the hill, there is a non-electric bakery. In the morning you're invited to stop in for fresh donuts and coffee.

Countryside Camper's Paradise   (216) 893-3002 Mondays only (maybe)
4280 Township Road 356, Route 4
Millersburg, Ohio 44654 (south of Route 39 off State Route 557)
Handicapped access: gravel path and steps into cabins

GUGGISBERG CHEESE FACTORY

Just across the valley is the place where Baby Swiss cheese was created. They make it Monday through Friday, and you're invited to watch in the morning, as well as visit their store and purchase some to take home.

Guggisberg Cheese   (216) 893-2500
Route 4, State Route 557
Charm, Ohio 44654   Handicapped access: yes

CHALET IN THE VALLEY RESTAURANT

Across the street from the cheese factory is another of the Guggisberg family enterprises: an authentic Swiss chalet that serves Swiss, Austrian, and Amish foods. There is also a bakery on the premises. During tourist season this is a very busy place, and the wait for a table can be up to an hour at lunchtime.

Chalet in the Valley   (216) 893-2500
Route 4, State Route 557
Charm, Ohio 44654   Handicapped access: yes

SLEIGH RIDES AND HAYRIDES

Another enterprise of the Guggisberg family is just up the road, where son Eric and his wife, Julie, have opened an inn. It offers whirlpool bathtubs in some rooms and includes packages that give you and a loved one a horse-drawn sleigh ride (when there is snow on the ground). In warmer weather, a horse-drawn Amish buggy takes you on a tour of the surrounding farms.

Guggisberg Swiss Inn   (216) 893-3600
P.O. Box 1, State Route 557
Charm, Ohio 44617   Handicapped access: yes

A CHARMING BED AND BREAKFAST

An Amish and Mennonite family operate a bed and breakfast on State Route 557. The building is new and set back from the road among the trees, with a great view of the pasture where cows and horses graze. The building is air-conditioned, and has electricity. Each room has a private, modern bath, and many of the quilts on the beds were made by family members. The breakfast is more like an Amish feast. If you are a big eater, you will love this place. There are 15 rooms and reservations are a must!

The Charm Countryview Inn Bed and Breakfast   (216) 893-3003
P.O. Box 100, State Route 557
Charm, Ohio 44617   Handicapped access: yes

A HILLTOP BED AND BREAKFAST

This is also a brand new bed and breakfast, built on the highest spot in Holmes County and offering a breathtaking view of the Amish country-side. The owners raise miniature horses and goats. Each of the nicely ap-pointed bedrooms has a private bath. The breakfast served here is no wimpy "continental-style" juice and roll; it's a full-blown Amish break-fast that includes homemade rolls and eggs and ham and other things. As at most popular inns, you must make reservations here well in advance.

Millerhaus Bed and Breakfast   (216) 893-3602
P.O. Box 126
Charm, Ohio 44617

A FOUR-DIAMOND INN

In Walnut Creek, the Dutch Corporation, which owns the original Amish-style restaurant in town, has built a beautiful hilltop inn that recently received an automobile club's prestigious four-diamond award. Some of the beautifully decorated suites have whirlpool baths for two, balconies overlooking Amish farms, and a country am-biance that is hard to describe until you stay there. The inn, which just opened in 1994, is very busy and reservations are a must.

Carlisle Village Inn   (216) 893-3636
P.O. Box 177
Walnut Creek, Ohio 44687   Handicapped access: yes

SMELLS GOOD AND TASTES GOOD

There really is a Mrs. Kaufman, who made the Mrs. Kaufman's Jams and Jellies that you find across Ohio at farm markets and stores. Her daughter continues the business and still makes the jams and jellies, small batch by small batch, in a modest building at the rear of her home. Stop in when she's open and you can watch. There's no charge for the wonderful smell.

Mrs. Kaufman's Jams   (216) 893-3278
3483 State Route 39 West
Walnut Creek, Ohio 44654   Handicapped access: steps into building

A LOOK AT AN AMISH HOME

If you are curious about the lifestyle of these hardworking people who shun modern life, you can peek behind their curtains without invading their privacy at Yoder's Amish Home, near Walnut Creek. Eli Yoder was raised Amish and many of his family are still members of the faith. The home and farm they have opened to the public was once owned by an Amish family, and many of the guides who work at the farm today are Amish. You can see both an old-fashioned Amish home and a more modern one that includes many non-electric appliances that may surprise you—including freezers and refrigerators. Rides in authentic Amish buggies are available, and locally-made quilts and crafts are for sale.

Yoder's Amish Home   (216) 893-2541
State Route 515
Walnut Creek, Ohio 44654   Handicapped access: yes, but gravel paths and steps into homes

31 Frank Takes a Ride

IT WAS A BRUTALLY COLD winter day. The temperature was hovering near the zero mark. It was perfect weather for a ride on Ohio's longest and fastest toboggan slide.

East Sparta, Ohio, south of Canton, is home to Bear Creek Camp Grounds. Once the temperature starts staying near the 40-degree mark, Bear Creek is able to start the refrigeration equipment that freezes the toboggan chute. The chute stretches for nearly a half-mile. You ride a truck to the top of a 250-foot-high hill at the back of the property, where a small two-story building is located. On the second floor is a platform that stretches out over the chute. You place your toboggan on this platform and then, when you are ready, an attendant drops the front of the platform, plunging you down one story onto the frozen chute. During the ride to the bottom of the 250-foot slope, you reach speeds of up to 70 miles per hour.

In case you are unable to stop when you reach the end of the chute, there is a 30-foot-long bed of straw and, beyond that, a stack of baled straw to stop runaway toboggans.

This is, quite simply, one of the most exciting outdoor rides in Ohio.

On the day we were taping our story, sending me up and down the toboggan run, we were alerted to a birthday celebration that was about to take place.

An elderly gentleman named Frank was about to take his first ride on the icy chute to celebrate his 90th birthday.

I asked Frank if he objected to our taping his ride. He did not. I asked him why he had chosen such an unusual way to mark his 90th year.

"I've always wanted to slide down that hill," he said, adding, "I thought I had do it pretty soon or forget it."

Frank also pointed out that he wasn't going down the hill alone. His neighbor was going to ride with him. His neighbor was 87!

We watched as the pair was trucked to the top of the hill and their toboggan carried into the little shed and up to the second floor.

By straining our eyes we could just see Frank and his neighbor climb aboard the toboggan, and we started our camera rolling.

The toboggan dropped and came flashing down the hill. The track was exceptionally slick that day and they reached top speed quickly.

When they came by our camera position, nearly three-quarters of the way down the chute, they whipped by us at such a great speed we were unable to focus on them.

We wheeled around just in time to see them reach the end of the chute, slice through the 30 feet of straw and slam head-on into a pile of baled straw. Both men tumbled off the toboggan.

Everyone was running towards them. Frank's neighbor was getting up, but Frank was still not moving. He was just lying there on his side, beside the capsized toboggan.

Several people were calling to him.

"Frank! Frank! Are you all right?"

Frank opened his eyes and said,

"Is it over yet?"

Later I asked Frank if he was planning to take another ride.

"Not until I turn 100!" he answered.

Bear Creek Resort	(216) 484-3901
3232 Downing Street, S.W.	Toboggan runs when weather permits
East Sparta, Ohio	Handicapped access: steps to launching area

A TEA ROOM AND RESTAURANT

In nearby Navarre, there's a quaint little restaurant where you can have a cup of tea, some wonderful homemade desserts, and the specialty of the house: cheese soup. There is a nice gift shop adjoining the restaurant. It's a wonderful place to warm up after tobogganing.

Abigail's Tea Room and Gift Shop	(216) 879-2867
Lyon Cottage, Rochester Square	
Navarre, Ohio 44662	Handicapped access: steps into cottage

BED AND BREAKFAST IN A HISTORIC CABIN

For a spot to spend the night in this area and a dinner you won't soon forget, head south on I-77 to historic Zoar. One of the oldest cabins in the village, Cowger House Number 9, is a unique bed and breakfast that offers not only the charm of a frontier cabin bedroom but also a private bathroom. The real treat here, for an additional cost, is the special fireside dinner that the owners put on by reservation only. Not only is the food excellent, but there is also entertainment that I can't tell you about without spoiling the surprise. I will tell you that if you enjoy American history you will be telling your friends about this place.

Cowger House #9   (216) 874-3542
4th Street
Zoar, Ohio 44697   Handicapped access: steps to rooms on second floor

OHIO'S UNKNOWN SOLDIER

Ohio had only one Revolutionary War fort, and it was at Bolivar, just up the road from Zoar. Here you can find the remains of Fort Laurens. The Ohio Historical Society has a building on the site where you can see a slide presentation on the fort and its story. Nearby is a tomb that holds the remains of one of the defenders of the fort. His body was discovered about 20 years ago when a new driveway was being built at the site.

He was later re-interred in a granite tomb as Ohio's "unknown soldier."

Fort Laurens State Memorial   (216) 874-2059
Route #1
Bolivar, Ohio 44612   (Open seasonally)

PAN FOR GOLD

You can look for gold and, maybe, find it right here in northern Ohio. The Tuscarawas River, near Bolivar, has traces of gold in it and, while you may never get rich from the amount that you find, it's a lot of fun and very exciting when you find that first golden flake. A canoe livery at the river's edge offers a course in how to pan for the gold and supplies the pans for a nominal fee. They will also give you directions to sandbars in the river where traces have been previously found, and rent you a canoe. Or you can try your luck at a large tank full of river sand right beside the office. (I found three flakes of gold there worth perhaps a dollar!)

NTR Canoe Livery and Gold Panning   216-874-2002
Bolivar, Ohio 44612   Handicapped access: yes

32 Ohio's First City

MARIETTA WAS OHIO'S FIRST city, part of the Northwest Territory leading to the western frontier. It was settled because of its location at the confluence of the Muskingham and Ohio Rivers.

Today it wears its antiquity like a proud badge, still a small river city though it has been a favorite with tourists for years.

One man responsible for putting Marietta on the tourist maps is Captain Jim Sands of the Valley Gem Sternwheeler. For many years, his has been one of the last operating paddle-wheel boats in Ohio.

The Valley Gem gives visitors a chance to see what life on the river was like, to experience the slow, regal travel of the great sternwheelers. Captain Sands also takes the ship up the Muskingham and through the 150-year-old hand-operated locks at the Muskingham river dam. It's a wonderful trip on an autumn day, with both sides of the river painted in fall colors. He offers dinner cruises and even performs wedding ceremonies on his boat. Former President George Bush, Ohio Governor George Voinovich, and other celebrities have taken turns at the wheel in the pilot house high atop the boat.

A year ago, Captain Sands's efforts to bring tourists to his riverfront city paid off. Because the number of passengers he was serving grew each year, he traded in the old Valley Gem for a brand new ship nearly twice its size. Today, the new Valley Gem continues to explore the Ohio and Muskingham Rivers on a year-round basis with daily cruises in the spring and summer and charter dinner cruises during the winter months.

Valley Gem Sternwheeler   (614) 373-7862
Docked at Washington Street Landing
Mailing address: 123 Strecker Hill
Marietta, Ohio 45750   Handicapped access: yes

A COLA MUSEUM

This museum is a tribute to a Marietta man who loved Coca Cola so much that he built a museum to his favorite drink. You'll find early Coke advertising, signs, soft-drink machines, and even ice cold Coke—still in bottles. There is a gift shop where you can buy replicas of early advertising signs and other coke memorabilia.

Butch's Cola Museum   (614) 376-COKE
118 Maple Street
Marietta, Ohio 45750   Handicapped access: steps into building

FLAGS AND POLES

There is a unique business in this river town: a shop that sells nothing but flags and flagpoles. You can buy anything from a miniature American flag for a parade all the way up to a 40-foot aluminum pole and all the hardware to get Old Glory flying in front of your home or business.

American Flags and Poles   (800) 262-3524 or (614) 373-4262
R.R. #1, Box 43-C, Route 7
Marietta, Ohio 45750   Handicapped access: yes

A RIVERBOAT THEATER

The Becky Thatcher Riverboat Theater started life as a working sternwheeler. When many of the old riverboats began heading for the scrap dealers after World War II, some far-sighted Marietta residents saw the possibility of recreating a bit of river history by converting this old sternwheeler into a permanently docked theater and restaurant. Today, the theater offers authentic riverboat melodramas, as well as musical shows, during the summer and autumn tourist seasons. The restaurant on the upper deck offers fine foods and a wonderful view of the Muskingham River.

The Becky Thatcher Restaurant and Show Boat
237 Front Street   (614) 373-4130 (restaurant) (614) 373-6033 (theater)
Marietta, Ohio 45750   Handicapped access: yes
The restaurant is closed on Sunday, year-round; theater is seasonal

GARDEN GLOBE FACTORY

If you have ever lusted after one of those silver garden balls that sit atop a birdbath—you know, the kind a fortune teller might have—we've found the last place in America that makes them. You can buy seconds right here at the factory.

Marietta Silver Globe Manufacturing Company   (614) 373-4951
R.D.#4 Box 382   Closed Saturday and Sunday
Pinehurst (Marietta), Ohio 45750   Handicapped access: busy factory, gravel driveway

A VICE-PRESIDENT OF THE U.S. WAS BORN HERE

Charles Gates Dawes, an army general in the first World War and Vice-President of the United States under Calvin Coolidge, was born here in Marietta, in this building that today houses a women's club.

Dawes is also remembered for his song-writing abilities and the fact that one of his songs, "It's All in the Game," became a popular hit in the 1950s. Today, the Betsy Mills Club, named for Dawes's aunt, is a residence for young women. It also operates a restaurant that attracts many of the civic leaders of the town for lunch and dinner each day. It's open to the public.

Betsy Mills Club Dining Room   (614) 373-3804
Fourth and Putnam Streets
Marietta, Ohio 45750

SLEEP ON A STERNWHEELER

This is the only place in Ohio where you can actually sleep overnight on an authentic sternwheeler. The Claire-E is a retired work boat that has been converted into a floating bed and breakfast. How-ever, because of insurance requirements, when guests are on board the ship must remain docked. The boat offers three staterooms with a shared bath and nicely appointed living room (or main salon, as the riverboaters like to say). In the morning, you troop off the boat and up the dock to the nearby Levee House Restaurant, also operated by the boat's owner, where you get your breakfast.

Clair-E Sternwheeler Boat Bed and Breakfast   (614) 374-2233
127 Ohio Street
Marietta, Ohio 45750   Handicapped access: steps in and out of rooms on boat

LEVEE HOUSE CAFE AND RESTAURANT

This former warehouse has stood for more than a century facing the Ohio River. The current owner renovated it and made it into a unique restaurant specializing in gourmet cuisine. An herb garden right outside the front door is used by the chef in the summer months to add fresh flavor to his dishes. Also, in good weather, the tables on the patio are a great place to have a glass of wine and watch a sunset on the Ohio River.

Levee House Cafe and Restaurant   (614) 374-2233
127 Ohio Street
Marietta, Ohio 45750   Handicapped access: yes

A PASTA FACTORY

You can watch gourmet pasta being made in this small riverfront factory. The pasta is shipped all over the U.S. and is a favorite of celebri-ties including Frank Sinatra. The factory store offers all the different varieties made here, as well as sauces to go with them, and recipes.

Rossi Pasta Factory   (614) 373-5155
114 Greene Street
Marietta, Ohio 45750   Handicapped access: yes

CAMPUS MARTIUS MUSEUM AND OHIO RIVER MUSEUM

The Campus Martius Museum houses the home of Rufas Put-nam, one of the founders of Marietta. It also has a good collection of exhibits on the early history of native Americans and the founding of the Northwest Territory. The Ohio River Museum, a block away, is a treasure trove of Ohio River boating history. Both are operated by the Ohio Historical Society.

Ohio River and Campus Maritus Museums   (614) 373-3750
Washington and Second Street
Marietta, Ohio 45750   Handicapped access: yes

From My Mailbag...

Dear Mr. Zurcher,

My husband and I would like To go To ThaT fanTasy hoTel you Told abouT on TV. The one ThaT had The dungeon and The cave-like rooms. Do you know if They give discounTs To senior ciTizens?

--Anxious in Bedford

33   A Train from the Past

SUGARCREEK WOULD BE a delightful place to visit because of its Swiss heritage. The entire town has been decorated like a Swiss village, with a facade on each business place resembling that of a Swiss chalet. Even the pay phone standing on a corner in the downtown looks like a miniature chalet.

As in many small towns, there is a small, neat, brick railroad station here. But unlike the abandoned stations of other small towns, the one here in Sugarcreek still plays host to thousands of passengers each year. This is the headquarters of the Ohio Central Railroad.

The Ohio Central is not your ordinary tourist train. It's an honest-to-gosh working small-line railroad that hauls freight from these small towns out to the Conrail and Chessie System lines. But on weekdays and Saturdays during the spring, summer, and fall, it also hauls passengers over an eight-mile stretch between Sugarcreek and Baltic. The line runs right through some of the most scenic Amish farms in the state, and the train is pulled by an antique steam locomotive—not sometimes, but almost every day.

You don't even have to have reservations. Just stop by the ticket office in the depot and you can pick up a ticket for one of the four runs made each day.

What adds to the enjoyment of the ride is that several of the conductors are members of the Mennonite faith. They can answer many questions about the Amish-Mennonite lifestyle and are very knowledgeable about tourist attractions in the area.

Ohio Central Railroad   (216) 852-4676
P.O. Box 564, 111 Factory Street
Sugarcreek, Ohio 44681   Handicapped access: steps into railroad cars

A MUSEUM OF CHEESE

They celebrate cheese in this town because it is one of the staples of life here. This tiny museum on the main street shows, in specially prepared rooms, how early cheese-making was done. It also offers a peek into the past of this community with a nice display of local memorabilia and early vehicles.

Alpine Hills Museum

Alpine Hills Museum   (216) 852-4113
106 West Main Street
Sugarcreek, Ohio 44681   Handicapped access: yes

SLEEP IN A BARN

You can literally sleep in a barn here in Sugarcreek, albeit a luxurious barn.

Sitting on a hilltop just outside of town is a bed and breakfast located in what was once a working Amish barn. Where hay was once stored, today there are rooms with cable TV, small balconies, modern bathrooms, and—are you ready for this—satin sheets on the bed. The bed and breakfast also offers Sunday night dinner to its guests because most of the other restaurants in the area are not open on Sunday.

The Barn Bed and Breakfast   (216) 852-2337 or 852-BEDS
Route 1, Box 1, County Road 70, P.O. Box 454
Sugarcreek, Ohio 44681   Handicapped access: steps to some rooms

A CARVER'S DELIGHT

A member of a famous carving family has brought his talents to the Sugarcreek area. David Warther, grandson of famed Dover carver Ernest "Moony" Warther, has opened his studio to the public.

David has dedicated his life to the history of sailing ships, much as his grandfather did to the history of steam engines. David already has completed a large number of exquisite ivory ships that trace the beginnings of ships powered by wind—from Biblical times to this century. The models are not for sale, but all are displayed to be enjoyed by visitors.

David Warther Carvings   (216) 852-3455
Route 2, Box 262A
Sugarcreek, Ohio 44681   Handicapped access: yes
Located in Dutch Valley Shops 1/2 mile east of Sugarcreek on State Route 39.

Warther Carvings

A MAGICAL PLACE

What could be more magical than a music box store that carries music boxes from all over the world?

Here you can find tiny, hand-carved boxes from the Black Forest, as well as new electronic ones that resemble circus sideshow rides. It is a pleasant place to visit even if you don't buy anything.

Music Box Chalet   (216) 852-3232
108 West Main Street
Sugarcreek, Ohio 44681   Handicapped access: steps into building

FOOD THE AMISH WAY

There are several Amish-style restaurants in and around Sugar-creek. This one is operated by the same firm that owns Der Dutch-man in Walnut Creek. They serve the traditional Amish fare of beef, turkey, and ham with lots of mashed potatoes, gravy, stuffing, a large salad bar, homemade bread, and pies—all for a reasonable price. Most everything is made fresh each day in the kitchen. There is also a bakery in-house so you can take home some of those Amish goodies.

Dutch Valley Restaurant　　　　　　(216) 852-4627
State Route 39, East　　　　　　　　Closed on Sundays
Sugarcreek, Ohio 44681　　　　Handicapped access: yes

Sugarcreek, Ohio

REAL KETTLE-COOKED POTATO CHIPS

This is a tiny potato chip company just outside of Sugarcreek where they still make potato chips by hand in huge kettles. The product is then packaged and marketed under several different names, including Tripp's Chips and J.R.'s Chips. If you call ahead and they're cooking that day, they will usually invite you in to watch and sample some fresh hot potato chips. They usually cook the chips very early in the morning.

Tripp's Chips　　　　　　　　　(216) 852-2827
Ragersville, Ohio 44681　　Handicapped access: narrow aisles between cookers

CRAFTS AND MORE CRAFTS

An old hardware store on the edge of town has taken on new life as the home of local artists and craftspeople. More than 130 of them are represented here, selling everything from homemade wooden pitchforks to intricate Amish quilts. There are paintings, knick-knacks, and even a sturdy children's farm wagon, crafted by an Amish entrepreneur who makes his living building horse-drawn manure spreaders for his neighbors. You can shop here every day but Sunday. Credit cards are welcome, as is cash.

Artisan's Mercantile of Sugarcreek　　　(216) 852-2456
110 Andreas Drive
Sugarcreek, Ohio 44681　　　　　Handicapped access: yes

From My Mailbag...

Dear Mr. Zurcher,

I am writing to complain about the directions you gave on TV. You said I should take Interstate 77 from Cleveland but you didn't tell us where Interstate 77 is.

--Lost in Parma

34 The Longest Ride

THIS IS ONE OF MY FAVORITE Ohio secrets. A tiny, community-operated amusement park tucked away in a city park that offers what must be the longest merry-go-round ride in America.

Tuscora Park in New Philadelphia has had a tradition for generations of giving youngsters their money's worth when they climb aboard the carousel at the park. The ride usually lasts five minutes or more. The folks who operate it say that in recent years they have started cutting back on the time, because after going around and around for five minutes, many youngsters got so dizzy they became sick to their stomachs!

The carousel is a Spillman, made in New York, and it has been in constant use at Tuscora Park since 1940.

In addition to the merry-go-round, the park also offers several other attractions, including a ferris wheel, miniature train, small roller coaster, and some kiddy rides. The park also holds the city's swimming pool and picnic area. Open May–Labor Day.

Tuscora Park   (216) 343-4644
161 Tuscora Avenue, N.W.
New Philadelphia, Ohio   Handicapped access: yes

THE WARTHER LEGACY

In the 87 years of his life, Ernest "Moony" Warther left more than 60 intricate wood carvings as his legacy. Warther, who went no further than the second grade in school, did the carvings with no formal training, yet some of the foremost carvers in the world have proclaimed him as "The Master Carver."

He carved many things, but his most famous carvings show the history of steam engines, including a made-to-scale, eight-foot-long replica of Abraham Lincoln's funeral train done entirely of ebony and ivory. He was working on his 64th carving when he died in 1973.

Today, Warther's sons and grandsons carry on the knife business he started, and his carvings are still on display in the family museum.

Warther's Carving Museum   (216) 343-7513
331 Karl Avenue
Dover, Ohio 44622   Handicapped access: yes

TRUMPET IN THE LAND

This distinguished outdoor drama was among the first outdoor theater presentations in Ohio. Paul Green's Trumpet in the Land celebrated it's 25th anniversary in 1994. Thousands have come to an amphitheater just on the outskirts of New Philadelphia to see the story of Moravian Missionary David Zeisberger and his attempts to keep peaceful Native Americans out of the battle between the British and the American colonists during the Revolutionary War. His efforts ended in a tragic massacre of the Native Americans. The play runs from late June through Labor Day each summer.

Trumpet in the Land Outdoor Drama   (216) 364-5111
P.O. Box 450
New Philadelphia, Ohio 44663   Handicapped access: yes

Trumpet In The Land Outdoor Drama

SCHOENBRUNN VILLAGE

After you see Trumpet in the Land, you may want to see some of the places that figured prominently in the drama. One of them, Schoenbrunn Village, is nearby. This was the village founded by David Zeisberger and his Christian Indians. The homes, the school, and the church have all been re-created. Costumed interpreters tell the village's story when it is open (during the summer months, from Memorial Day until Labor Day).

Schoenbrunn Village   (216) 339-3636
State Route 259
New Philadelphia, Ohio 44663   Handicapped access: yes

GNADENHUTTEN

This is probably the town with the most often mispronounced name in the state. It was in Gnadenhutten that the tragic incident happened on which the play Trumpet in the Land was based. In 1782, an American militia massacred 96 Christian Indians because they refused to take sides in the Revolutionary War. Today, you can see the mass grave as well as a replica of the cabin where the killing occurred.

Gnadenhutten Historical Society   (614) 254-4143
Gnadenhutten, Ohio 44629   Handicapped access: yes

From My Mailbag...

Mr. Zurcher,

You were Talking abouT a "One Tank Trip" To Canada lasT nighT on TV. Will iT be abouT The same disTance iF I Take my car?

--Sandusky, Ohio

35 The Ohio Valley

IF THERE IS A BIT OF A RIVERBOAT gambler in you, if you love country music, if you like the beauty of hills and rivers, then where Ohio meets West Virginia is the place for you.

We'll start just across the river in Wheeling. Located here are the legendary Capitol Theater and Jamboree U.S.A., a program of country music that has been broadcast for more than 50 years on radio station WWVA and is second only to Nashville's Grand Ol' Oprey in longevity. Saturday nights find some of the top names in country music gracing the stage in downtown Wheeling.

Jamboree U.S.A   (800) 624-5456 or (304) 232-1170
Capitol Theater
Wheeling, West Virginia 26003   Handicapped access: yes

HERE COMES SPUNKY

For the gambler, there is Wheeling Island, in the middle of the Ohio River. Here, the greyhounds run year-round. This is also the home of one of West Virginia's first electronic gambling casinos. However, don't go looking for roulette wheels or dice tables; offered instead are more than 300 electronic machines that play blackjack, keno, and poker. You must be at least 18 years old to enter the casino, which is open every day—even when the dog track is not.

The track clubhouse has a restaurant where you can dine while watching and betting on the dog races. The food is above average for a place that has a captive audience, and the prices are moderate.

Wheeling Downs Race Track   (304) 232-5050
Wheeling Island
Wheeling, West Virginia 26003   Handicapped access: yes

DINNER ON THE RIVER

A great way to see downtown Wheeling, West Virginia is on a sternwheeler riverboat. The Valley Voyager has called Wheeling home for the last 10 years and offers year-round cruises on the Ohio River, as well as dinner and lunch trips, and even an occasional bingo cruise (the proceeds going to a local church). The boat is both heated and air-conditioned. There is usually entertainment on board. The food is catered by the boat's owner, who also operates one of the better restaurants in the Wheeling area. The ticket office for the ship is located in an old yellow railroad caboose parked beside the river near the Civic Center in downtown Wheeling.

Valley Voyage Sternwheeler   (800) 237-1867
P.O. Box 174
Wheeling, West Virginia 26003   Handicapped access: yes

OGELBAY PARK

One of the truly beautiful areas of West Virginia, Ogelbay Park, has something for just about everyone in the family. There are three professional golf courses, a mountaintop lodge and cabins, West Virginia's only zoo, hiking trails, beautiful gardens, museums, paddleboats, swimming pools . . . and the list goes on.

During the Christmas holidays, more than two million lights illuminate this mountaintop park, and each evening thousands of cars and buses from three states roll up and down the park roads.

Ogelbay Park   (800) 624-6988
State Route 88
Wheeling, West Virginia 26003   Handicapped access: yes

RENT A CAMP

Back on the Ohio side of the river there is a unique state park where you can try camping without spending much money. Barkcamp State Park's Rent-a-Camp program provides a family with a walled tent for the night, along with cots, lantern, cooler, cook stove, picnic table, and even a broom to clean up with. All you have to bring along is your blankets and food. It costs less than 20 dollars a night. The rent-a-camp program is available at several state parks throughout Ohio.

Barkcamp State Park contains more than 1,000 acres of land and has a 117-acre stocked fishing lake. There are 176 campsites on the property available to campers on a first-come, first-served basis. There is also a 700-foot-long public beach with picnic shelters.

Barkcamp State Park   (614) 484-4064
65330 Barkcamp Park Road
Belmont, Ohio 43718   Handicapped access: yes

Rent-a-Camp

A POPULAR EATING PLACE

They come from three states to eat at this cafeteria on U.S. Route 40, just outside of St. Clairsville, Ohio. Mehlman's has been in business for more than three decades. Everything they serve is made daily from scratch: fresh soups, breads, pies. They offer dozens of entrees ranging from meat loaf to baked steak.

Lines of hungry customers usually stretch out the front door on weekends. But the line moves surprisingly fast, and usually customers wait no more than 20 or 30 minutes to reach the serving tables. Prices are moderate, and because everything is priced a la carte, you can order just what you want.

Mehlman's Cafeteria   (614) 695-1000
U.S. Route 40 at I-70
St. Clairsville, Ohio 43950   Handicapped access: yes

GLASS CRAFTSMEN

One of the last of the glass-cutting craftsmen, who once were found in abundance in this area, still operates his glass-cutting company and welcomes tourists to watch as he etches images of birds and artwork into fine crystal vases and plates. There is a factory store at the entrance to the workshop where you can purchase some of his work.

Sickles Glass Cutting Company   (614) 695-8208
45835 National Road West
St. Clairsville, Ohio 43950   Handicapped access: steps into shop, narrow aisles

36 A Romantic Getaway

EVERY ONCE IN A WHILE I discover a place that I don't want to share with others, a place I want to keep just to myself. This bed and breakfast in Cambridge, Ohio is just such a place.

It sits on the top of a hill at the end of a long, lonely gravel road. From the outside, it's not terribly imposing. Just a pleasant, modern ranch home that is surrounded by trees and nestled at the edge of an orchard. The owners, Jim and Vicky Goudy, originally planned for it to be their retirement home. It has a barn, a spring-fed lake, lots of pasture for their horses, and privacy—lots of privacy. Their nearest neighbor is almost a mile away.

Inside, they have constructed a guest wing with three bedrooms, each with its own private bath. There is even a private entrance from the driveway to the rooms. Each room is decorated in a different style using some of the family's antiques and collectibles. Fluffy white robes are laid on the bed in each room, as is a tray of Vicky Goudy's chocolate chip cookies. At the end of the hallway is a deck that leads to an outdoor whirlpool spa and a sauna. There is a large, octagon-shaped, glassed-in family room at one end of the home that overlooks the pastures and yards. This is where you can read or just curl up and watch the grass grow from a comfortable chair.

For an additional fee, you can go fishing in their lake, take a hayride around the farm or—my favorite—have a gourmet picnic with someone you love on a secluded hilltop overlooking miles of valleys and hills. Vicky prepares the entire picnic in several lunch baskets and they transport you and the food to the picnic area. You arrange for a time you want them to come back to get you. They leave you alone with just the birds, the clouds, and, perhaps, a few wild deer for company. In the autumn, this is one of the most beautiful spots in Ohio.

Because of the limited number of rooms, reservations are absolutely necessary.

Misty Meadow Farm Bed and Breakfast   (614) 439-5135
64878 Slaughter Hill Road
Cambridge, Ohio 43725 Handicapped access: Some small steps in house

FACTORY TOURS AND GLASS FACTORIES

Cambridge has always been known for its glass industry and, in recent decades, for decorative glass. Perhaps its most famous product was Degenhart Glass. The company, now known as the Boyd's Crystal Art Glass, continues many of the famous products and develops new ones each year. They also offer tours of their glass-making plant, where you can watch artisans at work molding and blowing glass. There is a factory outlet store where you can buy their products.

Boyd's Crystal Art Glass (614) 439-2077
P.O. Box 127, 1203 Morton Avenue
Cambridge, Ohio 43725 Handicapped access: yes

OHIO'S BIGGEST BAKERY

This bakery claims to have the largest single store in Ohio. If it's baked, you can probably find it here, along with some of their award-winning trail bread. Their monster-cookies are as big as a pizza pie, and a unique birthday cake department features two portrait artists who can duplicate a photograph with cake icing to create a birthday-cake portrait of the person being honored.

Kennedy's Cakes and Donuts, Inc. (614) 439-2800
875 Southgate Parkway
Cambridge, Ohio 43725 Handicapped access: yes

OUTLET STORE FOR GLASSWARE

One of West Virginia's leading glass companies also has a factory outlet store here where you can buy factory seconds as well as some of their first-grade discontinued items. All of these can be had at a considerable savings over new merchandise in retail stores.

Fostoria Glass Outlet Store (614) 439-3600
Deer Creek Complex, Southgate Parkway
Cambridge, Ohio 43725 Handicapped access: yes

OUTDOOR DRAMA

One of Ohio's pioneer outdoor dramas is performed here. The Living Word, the story of Christ and his crucifixion, is staged in an outdoor amphitheater that creates a feeling of realism as the story unfolds. While most of the cast is made up of local volunteers, the performance has been well-received down through the years. The play is only shown on Thursday, Friday, and Saturday evenings during summer months. Call for times and dates.

The Living Word Outdoor Drama   (614) 439-2761
6639 Klass Road
Cambridge, Ohio 43725   Handicapped access: yes

CONEY ISLAND RESTAURANT

Don't let the name fool you. The Coney Island Restaurant did start out in life as a hot-dog stand, but that was long ago, before a fire destroyed the original place. The new restaurant still sells the famous "Coney Island" dogs, but they also have turned it into a full-scale family restaurant that has become a favorite stop for tour groups. The place is also known for its pies, made fresh every day. While they don't offer tablecloths or six forks and four knives at every place setting, this is a good place to take the kids for some home-cooked, plentiful servings.

Coney Island Restaurant   (614) 432-3878
632 Wheeling Avenue
Cambridge, Ohio 43725   Handicapped access: yes

OHIO POWER LANDS

The Ohio Power Lands is a good example of what can be done with some land that was once strip-mined. Today, 350 lakes stocked with fish dot 30,000 acres of reclaimed land. Picnic areas in shaded groves overlook meadows of wildflowers. There are hiking trails and primitive camping areas open to the public. The area is also open for hunting and trapping. All of this is free; just write for information on how to obtain the free use pass.

Ohio Power Lands
Ohio Power Company, P.O. Box 328
McConnelsville, Ohio 43756   Handicapped access: yes

37 **From the Wright Brothers to the Moon**

OHIO'S CONTRIBUTION TO AVIATION is unparalleled in the world. Not only were the Wright Brothers, who first proved man could fly with a powered aircraft, born here; the Buckeye State is also the birthplace of John Glenn, first American to orbit the earth, and Neil Armstrong, the first human to walk on the moon. If a group of Dayton-area enthusiasts had their way, the motto, "Ohio, the heart of it all" would be replaced by the slogan, "Ohio, birthplace of aviation."

If you would like to see and experience what it was like to fly in the days of the Wright Brothers, head down to Miamisburg, Ohio and sign up for a flight in the "Wright B Flyer." This is as close a replica to the original Wright Brothers' first commercial aircraft as modern aviation regulations will allow. You sit on an open wing, just as the first army pilots did. The two propellers are driven by a single huge bicycle chain. The contraption looks more like a box kite than an airplane.

The plane was built by a group of aviation professionals who wanted to re-create the army's first aircraft in such a way that they could actually fly it. While they have substituted some modern steel rigging for the original piano wire and added a transponder and radio to keep federal officials happy, the craft still looks and flies like the original.

For a donation of $125 you can sign up to take a flight in the "Wright B Flyer." You must sign a release; then you are escorted to the aircraft and helped to a seat on the wing beside the pilot. You are offered a pair of goggles, since there is no cabin and no windshield on the plane. The two propellers are behind you. Once they fire up, conversation is very difficult. You taxi to the end of the runway and start your takeoff roll. It hardly seems that you are going fast enough when the plane gently drifts into the air.

Flying the plane, as one pilot put it, is "like driving a tractor across a freshly plowed field." The flight consists of a straight-ahead course at an altitude of about 200 feet for a distance of roughly a thousand feet (higher and farther than the Wright Brothers' flew on their first flight). Then you land and are taxied back to the hanger, where you can pose for pictures in the plane and receive a certificate that tells the world you flew in same aircraft that taught the world to fly.

Weather permitting, the flights are scheduled, by reservation only, on Thursday through Sundays. The hangar, which is also a replica of the Wright Brothers' early hangar, serves a dual purpose: storage space for the aircraft, and a museum and giftshop of early flight memorabilia. They are currently restoring a Lockheed airplane cockpit similar to the one flown by Amelia Earhart at the time of her disappearance.

Wright B Flyer, Inc.   (513) 885-2327
10550 Springboro Pike
Miamisburg, Ohio 45342   Handicapped access: yes, to museum; steps onto airplane.

THE BIRTHPLACE OF MOONWALKING

The man who made the "one small step for man, one giant leap for mankind," Neil Armstrong, first man to walk on the moon, was raised in Wapakoneta, Ohio. Today, a moon-shaped building that seems to be rising from a mound along Interstate 75 is a museum dedicated to Armstrong's history-making voyage.

Inside, you will find the small airplane in which he learned to fly. There are pictures and memorabilia that trace his life from small-town Ohio to outer space. Also on display are personal items that he took with him to the moon, and there is a theater where a film of the most-watched event in history is played over and over. There is also a gallery of news headlines from around the world and copies of awards and presentations given to Armstrong on his return to earth. A dramatic place to take a photo of the family is at the end of the sidewalk to the entrance to the museum. It resembles an airport runway leading to a rising moon.

Neil Armstrong Museum   (419) 738-8811
I-75 & Bellefontaine Road
Wapakoneta, Ohio 45895   Handicapped access: yes

Neil Armstrong Museum

A FLYING WOMEN'S MUSEUM

This is another little-known attraction in the Dayton area. This museum, dedicated to the contributions of women in aviation, features exhibits of pictures, books, and displays on early women aviators, from Amelia Earhart (her flying suit is here) through Sally Ride, the first American woman in space. Open Saturday only; other times by appointment.

International Women's Air and Space Museum   (513) 433-6766
26 North Main Street
Centerville, Ohio 45459   Handicapped access: steps to second floor

38 The Adventure of Finding a Motel

ON ONE OF OUR FIRST TRIPS—to Dayton to visit the U.S. Air Force Museum—videographer Bill West and I decided to stay overnight and do some more taping the next day. Since we had no reservations, we opted to look for a nearby motel when we finished for the day.

It was almost dark when we started our search and not far from the museum we spotted a sign that said, "OTEL." The "M" had burned out.

We tried the door to the office but it was locked. A clerk motioned us to the side of the building where there was a small window guarded by bulletproof glass and equipped with an intercom system.

A tinny voice asked if we had reservations. I replied that we didn't but were looking for two single rooms just for the night.

A metal drawer, like those in-all night gasoline stations popped out of the wall, hitting me in the stomach. Inside were two registration forms.

"That'll be forty dollars per room, each!" announced the tinny voice from the intercom.

Bill West, who had been studying the spray-painted graffiti on the walls of the motel and had pointed out an abandoned car in the parking lot, suggested at this point that perhaps we should look at one of the rooms before handing over our money.

The clerk looked slightly offended but agreed to meet us at the front door.

The three of us walked to a string of rooms located next to a large, smelly dumpster at the rear of the complex. The doors to the rooms had three dead-bolt locks each.

The clerk pulled a large ring of keys from his belt and started searching for keys to open the room. When the locks had been opened, he turned the handle but nothing happened. He finally put his shoulder against the door and gave a great push and the door swung open.

Inside was a metal-framed bed, a small table, two mismatched chairs, and a television set that looked as though it belonged in a museum.

I walked to the bed and sat down to check the mattress. I suddenly found my chin nearly on my knees as the bed sagged to the floor under my weight.

"I don't think we want this room," Bill West said as he helped me up off the bed.

"No problem," the clerk replied. "I show you another one. Much better."

He led us around the corner to a side of the motel hidden from the highway. There was a chained-in area with two very surly guard dogs pacing back and forth and growling at us.

"Uh, what are the guard dogs for?" I asked.

"Oh, we keep them in the office at night to discourage holdups," the clerk replied with a smile.

He led us to another room that also had the three locks on the door. This time the door sprung open as soon as the locks were released.

This room was decorated just as plainly as the other one. I walked to the bed, but this time I did not sit down. I just leaned down and pushed on the mattress.

It was like pushing on the floor. It was as hard as a rock. As I was straightening up I noticed several dead bugs, lying feet up, on the window sill and a few others, still living, scurrying for cover.

From the expression on Bill West's face he had seen them too and was already headed for the door. I followed him. The clerk pursued us down the driveway.

"How 'bout I give you a better price?" the clerk said.

"No!" we both answered.

He didn't give up.

"I give you both rooms for twenty dollars a night," he urged.

"No!" we answered.

"I make it fifteen dollars a night," he said.

We just kept on walking towards our car.

"Hokay," the clerk shouted after us, "I give you my best deal: ten dollars a night!"

We drove off, the clerk still standing in the middle of the driveway.

Some hours later we finally located rooms in a large chain motel.

About three o'clock in the morning there was a roar that brought me out of a sound sleep and to my feet. I stumbled to the door and peeked out.

There in the hallway were about a dozen outlaw bikers. One of them, on a motorcycle, had just won a bet that he could ride his motorcycle up the stairs and down the hall.

These days when we travel we always ask if there are any conventions going on at the motel and we always ask to see the room before we register.

U.S. AIR FORCE MUSEUM

The largest military aviation museum in the world, this is perhaps one of Ohio's best year-round attractions. It offers a spectrum of aviation history from the Wright Brothers through two world wars and Vietnm, and includes space exploration. There is an IMAX theater that puts you right in the pilot's seat. In the 10 acres of exhibits there are more than 200 aircraft on display.

My favorite spot at the museum is in the annex, reached only by bus from the museum. The annex is located on the other side of the runway and houses many additional aircraft, including those once used by U.S. presidents. Here you will find Harry Truman's "Independence," the "Columbine" used by Dwight Eisenhower, and planes once used by John F. Kennedy, Lyndon Johnson, and others. Several of the presidential aircraft are open, and you can walk through them and see what presidential travel was like.

One of the nicest things about the museum is that admission is free. There is a charge for the IMAX theater. Open seven days a week.

U.S. Air Force Museum   (513) 255-3284
Wright-Patterson AFB
Springfield Pike
Dayton, Ohio 45418   Handicapped access: yes

CARILLON HISTORICAL PARK

This may be one of the least-known attractions in Dayton. It is a 65-acre park hidden away near the river. Here, the Deeds Carillon, a huge bell tower that overlooks the park, offers concerts at various times during the year. There is also a small historical village that includes a 1905 Wright Brothers plane, a replica of their bicycle shop, a 97-year-old schoolhouse, and a number of other interesting buildings and displays. The park is closed November through April. There is an admission charge.

Carillon Historical Park   (513) 293-2841
2001 South Patterson Boulevard
Dayton, Ohio 45418   Handicapped access: yes, steps into some historical buildings

DAYTON'S EARLIEST RESIDENTS

A few years ago, while excavating for a sewage disposal plant in Dayton, workers uncovered an 800-year-old village. Today, "Sunwatch" has become a tourist attraction. While the village has been rebuilt, by the Dayton Museum of Natural History, the mystery of what happened to the original Native American residents of the village is still unsolved.

Sunwatch Archaeological Park   (513) 268-8199
2301 West River Road
Dayton, Ohio 45418   Handicapped access: yes

THE STORY OF THE CIVIL RIGHTS MOVEMENT

At nearby Wilburforce, you can see the story of the Civil Rights movement of the 1960s unfold in photos, exhibits, films, and recordings. Housed here is the Afro-American Cultural Center, which, besides the permanent exhibit on the Civil Rights movement, has constantly changing exhibits of paintings and other cultural activities.

National Afro-American Museum & Cultural Center   PH:(513) 376-4944
350 Brush Road
Wilburforce, Ohio 45384   Handicapped access: yes

TRAPSHOOTERS HALL OF FAME

Ohio may have more halls of fame than any other state in the nation. We celebrate the very best in football, inventors, broadcasters, rock musicians, and even trapshooters.

This is a national exhibit that preserves the memory of such trapshooters as Annie Oakley and famed composer John Philip Sousa, among many others. Here you can see the guns used by the enshrinees as well as photos of trapshooting championships. The hall is open Monday through Friday.

Trapshooters Hall of Fame, Inc.   (513) 898-1945
601 West National Road
Vandalia, Ohio 45377   Handicapped access: steps to museum

39 A Most Unusual Grocery Store

NO ONE WILL ACCUSE Jim Bonaminio of being conservative in his approach to the grocery business. Take the entrance to his store in Fairfield, Ohio, just outside of Cincinnati. In the summertime, the drive is lined with palm trees. Real palm trees. And at the entrance to the store is a jungle lake, filled with life-size fiberglass pink and blue hippopotami, giraffes, and other creatures of the jungle. There is even a waterfall.

Along the walk to the front door are six-foot-tall lollipops, also made of fiberglass in various colors.

Welcome to Jungle Jim's Grocery. One of the first things you spot walking into the store is a six-foot-tall stuffed lion, dressed like Elvis Presley. The animated figure bursts into one of Presley's songs every few minutes. Overlooking the checkout counter is an animated hippo playing a piano. Sometimes the clerks dress up in gorilla costumes to wait on customers.

If you see a man on roller skates rolling up and down the aisles, carrying a cap pistol and exchanging shots with stock boys one minute, helping a lady choose the freshest vegetables the next, you have just met "Jungle Jim" Bonaminio, the owner.

Jim Bonaminio grew up in Lorain County and began his career selling fruit and vegetables out of the back of his pick-up truck at busy intersections. Today he is considered one of the top independent grocers in America as well as one of the most innovative.

In his store you will find an espresso coffee bar where you can have a hot cup of the flavor of the day chosen from hundreds of of coffees from around the world. He has imported-foods from all parts of the globe and a wonderful bakery. He pioneered the olive bar idea for grocery stores (it's like a salad bar, but it features about a dozen different kinds of olive). His vegetable and fruit section covers nearly half the store and most of the produce is fresh from the farm. In short, it's the kind of grocery store most of us would like to have in our neighborhood.

So why all the weirdness? Bonaminio wisely points out that kids love to come to his grocery store and that children often influence where parents shop. He also notes that the palm trees and the waterfall all help people remember and talk about his store. While some of his competitors may call Jim Bonaminio crazy, he's laughing all the way to the bank.

Jungle Jim's Grocery	(513) 829-1919
5440 Dixie Highway	Open seven days a week
Fairfield, Ohio 45014	Handicapped access: yes

A NEW USE FOR OLD TRAIN STATIONS

Cincinnati has taken the beautiful, old, but abandoned Union Terminal and made it into an outstanding tourist attraction.

Today, it houses the Natural History Museum, the Cincinnati History Museum, and a huge state-of-the-art OMNIMAX movie theater.

In the natural history museum you can walk through a cave and a glacier. In the history wing you can stroll through Cincinnati's riverboat era; a life-size paddlewheel boat tied at a wharf is a popular display.

The OMNIMAX theater offers a 72-foot-high domed screen that wraps above and around the viewers to give a life-like effect to the movies.

The huge rotunda of the building has been maintained much as it was in its glory days. Massive murals still cover the walls. The old information center in the center of the rotunda today serves as a guest relations booth for the two museums and theater. With its shops, theaters, and restaurants, the museum center has something for everyone in the family.

Museum Center at Cincinnati Union Terminal
1301 Western Avenue
Cincinnati, Ohio 45203   Handicapped access: yes
(513) 287-7037 Natural History Museum
(513) 287-7043 History Museum
(513) 287-7016 Omnimax Theater

THE FIVE-STAR RESTAURANT

There are only 12 restaurants in the United States that have won the prestigious five-star rating from the Mobil Travel Guide. Only one of them is in Ohio.

Maisonette is a Cincinnati tradition for French and northern Italian cuisine served in an elegant setting. Dinner here is not just for eating. It is an experience, with all the tuxedoed servers hovering around you, presenting your meal, course after course. It's expensive, but if you try Maisonette during lunch you will find prices are about a third of what they are in the evening.

Maisonette   (513) 287-7782 FAX (513) 287-7785
114 East Sixth Street
Cincinnati, Ohio 45202   Handicapped access: yes (even though it's an
old building, they have portable ramps to accommodate wheel chairs).

A PRESIDENT WAS BORN HERE

William Howard Taft, the 27th president of the United States, was born in Cincinnati. He was the only man ever to serve as both president of the U.S. and as chief justice of the U.S. Supreme Court.

His birthplace has been restored by the National Park Service and is open to the public. The home had for many years been an apartment house and little was left of the original floor plan. The park service was able to restore it by using Taft's mother's letters to friends, in which she described the rooms, the wallpaper, and the furniture.

William Howard Taft National Historic Site   (513) 684-3262
2038 Auburn Avenue
Cincinnati, Ohio 45220   Handicapped access: yes

ABOUT THAT CINCINNATI CHILI

You can't come to Cincinnati without trying the chili for which the city is famous. Whether you have it three-way or four-way, it is a gastronomic experience. The chili, more like spaghetti with a cinnamon-flavored tomato sauce, is served with optional cheese, onions, and red beans. There are chili shops all over Cincinnati. The one we tried was perhaps the best known.

Skyline Chili
79 restaurants in Ohio, Kentucky, Indiana, and Florida; write:
4180 Thunderbird Lane   (513) 874-1188
Fairfield, Ohio 45014   Handicapped access: yes to most restaurants

A RIVERBOAT CRUISE

If you can't afford a cruise for a week or two on the Delta Queen, perhaps you can afford an afternoon on the Becky Thatcher or the Mark Twain, two of Cincinnati's paddlewheel tourboats.

It's a great way to see the Cincinnati skyline and learn a bit about the history of this famous riverport. They also offer lunch and dinner cruises.

B.B. Riverboats   (606) 261-8500
P.O. Box 1007
Covington, Kentucky 41012   Handicapped access: yes

WIENERSCHNITZEL AND BROADWAY

You can get a little of the German heritage of Cincinnati, as well as young professional singers presenting the latest and best of Broadway, at this most unique restaurant.

All the serving people are either advanced music students or professional singers. The restaurant serves authentic German food and, when the meal is done, the servers take to the stage to give the audience a rousing performance of the tunes from famous Broadway shows. The evening also includes a lot of audience participation. The food may be average German fare, but the entertainment is top-notch.

Forest View Gardens   (513) 661-6434 FAX (513) 661-5873
4508 North Bend Road
Cincinnati, Ohio 45211   Handicapped access: yes

SOME BARGAIN SHOPPING

Just outside of Cincinnati is a place that manufactures down-filled comforters for some of the major department and specialty stores in America. They have an outlet store at the factory where you can buy not only the comforters but other down-filled clothing as well. The best buys are the comforter seconds, which may have been rejected by the department stores because of a crooked stitch or mismatched fabric. You can usually save up to 50 percent on these items, but you have to ask for them.

Down-Lite International   (513) 489-3696
7818 Palace Drive.
Cincinnati, Ohio 45246

One Tank Tip #10

Don't Be a Dim Bulb

If you like to read in bed take along a 100-watt light bulb. Many hotels and motels use small wattage bulbs as an economy measure, making reading a chore.

40 Antique Capital of the Midwest

THE TINY COMMUNITY OF Waynesville, in Warren County, is only five city blocks long and has only one main street. Yet in those five blocks are packed nearly 40 antique shops with hundreds of antique dealers and their wares, making this community the "Antique Capital of the Midwest."

There was a Waynesville even before there was a state of Ohio. The village was founded in 1796, and many of the town's older buildings have been preserved.

The town also sponsors one of the stranger, but quite popular festivals in the state: The Ohio Sauerkraut Festival. Held for 25 years now, this festival is one of few places you'll find candy made from sauerkraut and even ice cream with a sauerkraut base!

What makes the festival stranger still is that the town is not known for raising cabbage, nor are many people here of German heritage. In fact, the idea for the festival grew out of a meeting by town merchants over ideas for a festival, and one merchant made the chance remark that he had just had sauerkraut for lunch and had enjoyed it. Why not sponsor a sauerkraut festival? They did, and the rest is pungent history.

The Village of Waynesville   (513) 897-8855 Fax: (513) 897-9833
Waynesville Chamber of Commerce
174 South Main Street, P.O. Box 281
Waynesville, Ohio 45068

WHEN KNIGHTS WERE BOLD

If you have ever fantasized about living in a time of knights and dragons, lords and ladies, you can live out your fantasy here in southwest Ohio.

The Ohio Renaissance Festival is now in its fifth year. For eight weekends each summer, a 16th-century English country fair comes to life in the rolling hills of Warren County, complete with a 30-acre village where knights in armor on horseback joust with spears and swords. There are court dancers and jesters, strolling minstrels, jugglers, and even serving wenches.

Craftspeople from around the country come to the festival to sell swords, clothing, glass-blown items, and even medieval-type foods. The festival runs from late August into October on weekends.

The Ohio Renaissance Festival   (513) 897-7000 FAX: (513) 897-7003
State Route 73, P.O. Box 596
Waynesville, Ohio 45068-0596

The Ohio Renaissance Festival

A REALLY BIG FLEA MARKET

On a nice summer weekend, nearly a thousand vendors can be found set up indoors and outdoors here at the intersection of I-71 and State Route 73. The permanent buildings can hold 500 dealers; hundreds more set up in the surrounding parking lots during the summer when the weather permits.

Open year-round on Saturday and Sunday.

Caesar Creek Flea Market
7763 State Route 73 West
Wilmington, Ohio 45177
(513) 382-1669

PARAMOUNT'S KINGS ISLAND AMUSEMENT PARK

One of America's most famous theme parks, King's Island has more than 350 acres of thrill rides, water park, shops, and restaurants. It is home of "The Beast," the world's longest wooden roller coaster; "King Cobra," America's first stand-up looping roller coaster; and "The Racer," a double-track wooden coaster with one train running forward and one running backward.

The "WaterWorks" is a 15-acre water park with 15 water slides, including inner-tube rides—guaranteed to get you very wet and cool you off on a hot Ohio summer's day.

Paramount's King's Island   (513) 573-5802 FAX (513) 573-5795
6300 King's Island Drive
King's Island, Ohio 45034

A ROMANTIC HIDEAWAY

We found this tiny cottage tucked behind a historic home in Lebanon. It's owned by an artist, who hand painted all the tiles in the kitchen, bathroom, and around the gas-fired fireplace.

There is an in-ground swimming pool just outside the door, and a hot tub nearby. The cottage, built in 1864, was once a carriage house before being converted to a bed and breakfast. It now has a kitchen, private bath, and loft bedroom.

The Artist's Cottage Bed and Breakfast   (513) 932-5938
458 East Warren Street
Lebanon, Ohio 45036   Handicapped access: yes

From My Mailbag...

Dear Neil,

I don't understand what a "One Tank Trip" is. Will I still be able to take the trips if I don't have a Tank?

--Wondering

41 But Never on Tuesday

ONE OF SOUTHWEST OHIO'S hidden gems is the historic Clifton Mill in Clifton, Ohio. It's the largest water-powered grist mill in the world still operating. The waters of the Little Miami River are diverted through the base of the mill, powering the grinding wheel much as it has been done for almost 200 years.

In addition to fresh-ground flour and meal, the mill also offers a gift shop which sells its product and other souvenirs.

There is a small restaurant where the breakfast fare is legendary. They make pancakes here. I mean they make real pancakes here. Pancakes that are almost the size of manhole covers. They boast that rarely can anyone finish a stack of three of their flapjacks. For dessert, if you are still hungry, they offer their signature oatmeal pie.

The mill really shines during the Christmas season. The day before Thanksgiving, they turn on more than two million lights that outline the mill, mill wheel, and adjoining valley. There is also a display of three thousand animated Santa Claus figures and a miniature copy of the village of Clifton that has electric trains and even an animated Christmas parade. There is also a Santa Claus workshop where a real Santa practices for the big night every 15 minutes by running up and down his chimney and waving to appreciative families watching from below.

Not surprisingly, at Christmastime the mill attracts thousands of people each evening. A sizable staff is required to serve the crowd and to keep people from wandering too close to the illuminated mill wheel or from falling into the valley of the Little Miami River, which runs through the grounds.

The lights are on at the mill each evening, except Tuesdays, until New Year's Day. On Tuesdays, the lights are out and the mill is closed. It says so in all their advertising. There are signs posted all around the front of the mill saying, "Closed on Tuesdays."

The first year that they lit the mill, Tony Santariano, the owner, put the lighting display on a timer so the lights came on promptly each evening at 6:00 p.m. and off at 9:30 p.m. On Tuesdays, he would just turn off the timer so the lights would not come on.

That year, Christmas happened to fall on a Tuesday, and so the mill was closed. Christmas night, Tony and two of his daughters were moving a canoe, which they had received as a gift, from their home to a storeroom in the darkened mill. However, when they pulled up to the street the mill is on, they found it choked with cars and people. It was about 5:45 p.m. Darkness had just fallen, and people were waiting to see the lights come on.

Tony tried to explain to the crowd that there would be no lights tonight, that the mill was closed on Tuesdays, and, for safety reasons, he could not turn on the lights because he had no staff. The crowd was not happy about this. In fact they became downright surly. They started to shout at Tony and his daughters. The trio, with their canoe, beat a hasty retreat inside the mill.

"Don't turn on any lights!" Tony warned his daughters, "If they see a light on, they'll think I changed my mind and that we're open."

He told one of his daughters to toss him the mill keys. He wanted to be sure the door was locked.

She tossed the keys, which went sliding under a counter. The three were searching the floor trying to find the keys in the blacked out room when suddenly:

"WHAM!"

The night was flooded with lights. Tony had forgotten to turn off the timer and all the thousands of lights outside had sprung to life.

The crowd of nearly 200 outside cheered and surged forward onto the grounds.

Realizing that the three of them could not control so large a crowd, Tony ran to the light switch and turned it off, plunging the mill into darkness again.

For the next half-hour Tony and his daughters huddled on the floor of the darkened mill as people pounded on the door, occasionally peeking out windows to see if the angry crowd had left.

The timer is now gone. Nowadays the lights are turned on manually, to burn Wednesday through Monday Nights. But never on Tuesday.

The Historic Clifton Mill   (513) 767-5501
75 Water Street   Closed on Tuesdays
Clifton, Ohio 45316   Handicapped access: steps into mill

THE LAST REAL DAIRY

Just a short distance from Clifton is perhaps the last dairy in Ohio to serve unpasteurized milk. Young's Jersey Dairy has been in business for decades, and when the law was passed requiring all milk to be pasteurized, they and other existing dairies were exempted. What this all means is that, while their milk meets all safety and health requirements, by being non-pasteurized—some say—it is easier to digest. It has natural vitamins A and D and contains some of the richest butterfat content of all milk still used in making ice cream.

In fact, Young's has become a tourist attraction. Their dairy farm is nextdoor to the store, and the barns are open to visitors. Kids can pet baby cows and goats, climb on tractors, and watch the milking operation.

Next door in the dairy, which is open 24 hours a day, they serve dozens of flavors of rich Jersey ice cream. There is also a bakery, a gift shop, and a small restaurant.

Young's Jersey Dairy   (513) 325-0629
6880 Springfield-Xenia Road
Yellow Springs, Ohio 45387   Handicapped access: yes

A COLLEGE TOWN BED AND BREAKFAST

This lovely old home near Antioch College is also within walking distance of downtown Yellow Springs. It has been made into a bed and breakfast that attracts many academicians who are visiting the college.

Morgan House Bed and Breakfast   (513) 767-7509
120 West Limestone Street
Yellow Springs, Ohio 45387   Handicapped access: steps to upper floors

CLIFTON GORGE STATE NATURE PRESERVE

You can find more than 300 kinds of wildflowers growing here, and more than 100 species of trees. The little Miami River has cut a 22-foot gorge through this park which, legend has it, Daniel Boone once leaped across in a bid for freedom after being captured by Native Americans. If you like to hike, there are four miles of challenging trails. The preserve is right next to John Bryan State Park.

Clifton Gorge State Nature Preserve   (513) 964-8794
Jackson Street
Clifton, Ohio 45316
or

Ohio Dept of Natural Resources   (614) 265-6453
1889 Fountain Square
Columbus, Ohio 43224

OHIO'S LARGEST OUTLET MALL

There are more than 75 stores in this new outlet mall, and more are on the way. You'll find everything from name-brand jeans to fine china. As with all outlet malls, not everything is a bargain. Watch for close-outs, discontinued stock, and seconds for the best prices.

Ohio Factory Shops   (614) 948-9090
8000 Factory Shops Blvd., (I-71 & Jeffersonville exit)
Clifton, Ohio 43128   Handicapped access: yes

From My Mailbag...

Neil Zurcher,

I understand you were advertising about a flea market. I don't know why anyone would want to buy fleas, but I have an old cat that has plenty to spare.

--Bugged in Cleveland Heights

Other States

42 Smokey in the Mountains

PHOTOGRAPHER JOHN PAUSTIAN and I had set out on a One Tank Trip to the Smoky Mountains of Tennessee. We had decided to see if we really could make it all the way there on just one tank of gasoline. We topped the car's gasoline tank as we left Cleveland and started south on Interstate 71. In the trunk we had stashed a two-gallon can of gasoline. Not that we doubted we would make it, but just to make sure we didn't have to walk in case our calculations were wrong.

We drove steadily, hour after hour, as counties gave way to state lines until we finally saw up ahead the magic words: Tennessee State Line. Our gasoline gauge was showing just about an eighth of a tank left. We drove on, carefully observing the 55 mph speed limit, wanting to nurse every mile, every yard, out of each drop of gasoline left. Finally we were at the Sevierville city limits. Our destination of Pigeon Forge, Tennessee was just one mile away. We were truly going to make it on one tank.

We were congratulating each other when the car suddenly died. A quick glance at the gasoline gauge showed no movement from the needle which rested against the "E" mark.

John, or J.P. as he liked to be called, swore under his breath.

"Better get the can out of the trunk," he said.

We were just coasting over the crest of a small hill when we spotted it at the bottom of the hill: an ESSO gasoline station.

"Might as well coast down there and fuel up," J.P. said.

We slowly crested the hill, then started downward. Our newscruiser was picking up speed as the hill unrolled beneath us. We were almost at the gasoline station and I was thinking how nice it would be to stretch my legs. Suddenly I realized we were driving right by the station.

"Hey!" I said, "What are you doing. Why don't you stop for gas?"

J.P. was hunched over the wheel, his eyes locked on something down the road.

Then I saw it, too, and started to cheer him on. Both of us were trying to use the power of concentration to urge our now-dead car the last half-mile to the sign that read: Welcome to Pigeon Forge.

We coasted closer and closer, but, at the same time, the road started to rise and our speed, already only a mile or two an hour, started to slow even further.

"No, you son-of-a-bitch!" J.P. shouted at the car. "You're not going to stop this close!"

He suddenly threw open the door, jumped out of the car, and, keeping one hand on the wheel to steer, began to push the car the last 50 feet. Realizing what he was trying to do, I did the same on my side. Gasping and pushing, we crossed the corporation line and pulled off to the side of the road. We had made it to our destination in Tennessee on one tank of gasoline.

It was this kind of determination that made J.P. such a joy to work with. But there were times his enthusiasm almost got us into trouble.

On the last morning of our stay in Tennessee I heard a buzzing sound. I thrashed around in the predawn darkness, groping around on my night stand for an errant alarm clock, only to realize that it was not a clock but my phone that was buzzing.

I snatched it off the stand and growled, "HELLO!"

"Good morning, it's time for magic!" J.P. answered brightly.

"What time is it?" I mumbled.

"Three a.m." he responded.

"Three a.m.!" I shouted back. "It's the middle of the night. Have you been drinking?"

"Come on, get out of bed," he urged. "It's almost Magic Time."

"What are you talking about?" I demanded.

"I want to get up in the Smokies to see the sunrise and capture all that great magical color in the early morning," he replied. "Besides, you said you wanted to see the real Smoky Mountains, and this is your chance."

The memory of my words haunted me as I stumbled around the motel room dressing, the sting of the cool mountain morning helping to bring me more awake as I crunched across the gravel parking lot, still illuminated by the moon, to our car.

A half-hour later we were starting the winding climb up the mountain roads into the Great Smoky Mountain National Park. The sky was turning to gold and purple in the east as we reached a lookout on the summit and pulled over.

J.P. was nearly dancing. He was like an excited child on Christmas morning. He leaped out of the car and yelled,

"Come on Zurcher! It's MAGIC TIME!"

It truly was magic as we stood, he looking through his camera and I watching, mesmerized by the rainbow of hues evolving out of the eastern sky as the first golden rim of the sun pushed up from behind the horizon. Even more beautiful was the river of white fog that drifted down the mountain valleys below us. It truly did look as though the mountains were covered with smoke.

"You only get this golden light for about a half-hour in the morning," J.P announced. "Come on, we've got to take advantage of it."

He started packing his tripod into the trunk of the car and wrestled his camera into the front passenger seat.

"Here, you drive," he said, flipping me the keys.

We had only gone a few hundred feet when he shouted, "This isn't going to work. Stop the car!"

I slammed on the brakes, barely in time, as he stepped out the door of the still moving car. The next thing I knew, he was climbing on the hood of the car, his back braced against the windshield.

"O.K!" he shouted. "I can see now, try to drive at a steady speed."

And so, down the mountain we came. Me driving, leaning out the side window to see where I was going. J.P. sprawled across the hood and windshield, chuckling and talking to himself. "That's beautiful! That's great!"

I noticed the tan pickup truck pass us, going in the opposite direction, and the startled face of the driver, but I was too busy trying to keep the car on the winding road and worrying about J.P. falling off and being run over by his own newscruiser.

Suddenly, I heard a siren. I snapped erect and looked in the rearview mirror. Behind me was the pickup truck, which now had a blue flashing light going on top of the cab, and the ranger behind the wheel was motioning me to pull over.

"I've got a cop behind me!" I shouted out the window to J.P. "He wants me to pull over."

"Not now," J.P. hollered back. "This is a great shot. Let me finish it, keep on driving."

"He looks pretty mad!" I shouted back. "I think I better pull over."

"No! Just keep driving for another couple of minutes while I finish this shot!" J.P. yelled.

So I kept driving until we rounded another bend and, where there was a wide berm on the road, I slowed, pulled off, and stopped.

J.P. lay back on the hood to relax, still euphoric about the beauty he had just captured on his camera. The ranger, about six-feet-four of him, came marching up to my window and said,

"JUST WHAT IN THEE HELL WERE YOU BOYS A-DOING?"

"It was magic, pure magic," J.P. answered, his voice still full of wonder, from the hood of the car.

"What in the hell is that boy talkin' about?" the ranger demanded of me. "Is he high on some kind of dope or somethin'?"

It took us several minutes and some identification to convince the ranger that we were indeed sober, and were just a couple of nutty journalists that had gotten carried away with the beauty of a Smoky Mountain morning.

My friend J.P., who could get so enthused about the beauty of a new day, left us a short time later, losing a valiant fight with cancer. He was only 37 years old.

There is a little less magic in the world without him.

WHAT WE FOUND BESIDE THE MOUNTAINS

Probably the other most noteworthy event in this trip was the day I flew like a bird!

Pigeon Forge, Tennessee is located at the base of the Smoky Mountain National Park and offers one of the most unusual tourist attractions in the country. It's called Flyaway.

Flyaway is a bit difficult to explain. From the outside it looks like a large grain silo. Inside is a round, tall room with a grid for a floor. Beneath the grid is a huge airplane motor and propeller that drives a wind of more than 150 miles per hour up through the floor. You don a skydiver's coverall, a helmet, and protective glasses and walk into the room with an instructor. If you do everything he tells you, you leap into the column of air and actually fly! Experienced skydivers can stay up 20 or 30 feet in the air for 15 or 20 minutes at a time.

How long did I fly? Probably about three miliseconds. But I flew. They do require everyone who tries this sport to first sign a release and watch a film explaining safety requirements and the principles of sky-diving. And first-timers go into the chamber with an experienced in-structor. Can you get hurt? Absolutely. It's like any other sport; if you don't do it right, you run the risk of injury. Is it fun? You bet. There is just no ride like it on earth outside of a free-fall from an airplane.

By the way, if you really don't want to fly, they do have a circular stairway around the cylinder where you can watch through port-holes as others fly.

Flyaway Indoor Skydiving   (615) 453-7777
519 North Parkway
Pigeon Forge, Tennessee 37863   Handicapped access: Good question. I don't
   know how to rate this one. Best call first and discuss your needs with them.

Flyaway Indoor Skydiving

OTHER THINGS TO DO

Pigeon Forge is home to one of the larger outlet malls in the country. If you are a careful shopper, you can find many major brand bargains here. But be aware: just because it's called an outlet store doesn't necessarily mean it offers prices lower than those in your local department store. In fact, the main advantage of outlet malls is that you can usually find a good selection of colors and sizes when it's a company-owned store. Ask for and look for seconds in the stores: these are usually the real bargains.

The Pigeon Forge Factory Stores   (615) 428-2828
North Parkway
Pigeon Forge, Tennessee 37738   Handicapped access: yes

Pigeon Forge Department of Tourism   1-800-251-9100
P.O. Box 1390G
Pigeon Forge, Tennessee 37863

From My Mailbag...

Dear Neil,

Are "One Tank Trips" only for humans, or can my dog and my mother-in-law go too?

--Separated in UnionTown

43 Peace on Earth and Goodwill to All

VIDEOGRAPHER BOB BEGANY and I had traveled to Charleston, West Virginia to do a holiday season One Tank Trip segment on the West Virginia state capital and their giant sternwheeler, the West Virginia Belle.

The idea was to get a nighttime shot of the Belle, all lit with holiday decorations as she sailed down the Kanawha River past the imposing state capitol building and towards downtown Charleston.

The first problem was that the boat moved faster than we had anticipated, so we appealed to one of the owners to accompany us with a walkie-talkie to a site on a college campus, directly across the river from the capitol building. The walkie-talkie was for communicating with the boat's captain to slow him down a bit while we got the camera set up.

We discovered the second problem when we arrived on the campus. All of the streetlights ended at the edge of a row of buildings a hundred feet back from the river's edge, which meant the last hundred feet to the river was in total darkness—and none of us had thought to bring along a flashlight.

The boat had already gone upriver and turned for its run past the capitol by the time we found a parking place and began running through inky blackness towards the river's edge.

Across the river, the West Virginia capitol glowed in the light of the moon that was just rising over a mountain behind the building. The lights of the capitol were reflected in the water and upriver we could see the merry lights of the approaching West Virginia Belle. The Captain told us by radio that he was going as slowly as he could, but a strong current was carrying him towards us.

In the darkness, Begany and I fumbled to set up his tripod and mount his camera. It was so dark that everything had to be done by touch. But in minutes the camera was locked on and the eyepiece with its tiny monitor was glowing.

It was going to be an absolutely beautiful picture. The Belle had Christmas carols cascading from her loudspeakers as she serenely glided down the river, all aglow, towards the capitol. Begany was just starting to focus in on the ship when, suddenly, his eyepiece went black.

Begany, who was renowned for his ability to curse, filled the air with expletives as he grappled in the dark with the battery container on the camera. He ripped it open and reached for his spare battery in his belt. I was urging him on as the ship got closer and closer.

In his haste to replace the battery he dropped it, just as I stepped closer to see if I could help. My foot accidentally hit the falling battery, booting it away into the pitch blackness of the night.

Begany's cursing hit a new fever pitch as we both dropped to our knees and started feeling around the grass trying to find the battery. The ship's officer, who had accompanied us, was trying to strike a cigarette lighter he had in his coat. The Belle was only minutes away from passing us.

"WHY ME LORD? WHY ME?" Begany implored, as we frantically moved from spot to spot trying to feel the battery.

Suddenly I had an inspiration. I jumped to my feet and called to the ship's officer with the walkie-talkie.

"Use your radio to call the ship and ask them to hit us with their spotlight!" I yelled.

Within seconds I could see crewmen running out onto the bridge of the ship to where the huge spotlights were mounted.

The night was suddenly shattered by a blinding white light. A million-candle-power spotlight froze us on the grassy lawn, the white glare momentarily blinding both Begany and myself.

Whatever hopes we had of finding the battery and saving our shoot were seemed gone in the flash. Fortunately, the ship's officer, anticipating the brightness of the lamp, had turned his back on it and, as the light blinded us, he scanned the ground and spotted our lost battery.

"HALLELUJAH!" shouted Begany as the man pressed the battery into his hand.

Just then the night was illuminated again, followed by a sharp explosion!

We had been so intent on watching the approaching boat that we did not notice the flashes of lightning to our rear, and as Begany scrambled to put the battery into the camera, the first drops of rain started to fall as the thunder rumbled. Within seconds it was pouring, and in the downpour we got one waterlogged shot of the West

Virginia Belle as it sailed past the capitol building and on towards downtown. In its wake, drifting back to us from the boat, we could hear, above the rain and Begany's swearing, the words to the old carol, "Peace on earth and good will to men."

Sadly, the West Virginia Belle has since moved on to the more lucrative service of riverboat gambling in another state, and only a much smaller tourist boat remains to give tourists that most impressive look at the West Virginia state capitol seen only from the water.

RIDE IN SANTA'S SLEIGH

If you visit downtown Charleston in the evening during the holiday season, you can take a ride with Santa in his sleigh. He leaves the reindeer back at the North Pole and instead uses a single horse while in Charleston. The sleigh is also equipped with wheels under the runners in case of warm weather and no snow. You can usually find the sleigh at the civic center downtown. For more information, contact:

Santa's Sleigh Ride   (304) 743-6861 or (304) 755-0427
P.O. Box 6
Milton, West Virginia 25541   Handicapped access: yes

RENT A FARM

If you want to get away from it all, then rent this mountaintop farm just outside of Charleston for a weekend or a week. Owned by a Charleston attorney, the historic farmhouse has been beautifully decorated and modernized and is used for weddings, reunions, anniversaries, and other occasions. It offers total privacy. A caretaker lives in a cabin near the entrance, and while he is available in emergencies, you are usually left completely alone.

Benedict Haid Farm   (304) 346-1054
Number 8 Hale St.
Charleston, West Virginia 25301 Handicapped access: some steps in house

ANOTHER PLACE TO PLAY THE DOGS

Charleston also has a relatively new greyhound racing track. Open year-round, it offers pari-mutuel betting and a casino with electronic game machines that play poker, keno, and blackjack.

Tri-State Greyhound Racing Park   (304) 776-1000
P.O. Box 7118
Cross Lanes, West Virginia 25301   Handicapped access: yes

YUGOSLAVIAN FISH STEW

I don't know why, but Charleston is famous for Yugoslavian fish stew. Rumor has it that some Yugoslavian fishermen visited here years ago and, longing for the food of their homeland, talked one of the restaurants into trying the recipe for the stew. It was so good that other customers started asking for it and today it is still served.

General Seafood Restaurant   (304) 343-5671
213 Broad Street
Charleston, West Virginia 25301   Handicapped access: yes

TO TOUR THE TOWN OR CAPITOL

Write or call the local convention and tourism bureau. They can provide you with maps and directions, as well as hotel and motel recommendations.

Charleston/Kanawha Convention and Visitors Bureau   (304) 344-5075
200 Civic Center Drive
Charleston, West Virginia 25301

One Tank Tip #11
Tool Up for a Quicker Bath
Carry along a pair of pliers to remove water savers on faucets in motels where the bathtub takes all night to fill. Be sure you replace whatever you remove before you leave.

44 Wings Over New York

ONE OF THE SKILLS I ACQUIRED over the years, as the result of a story, was the ability to fly a sailplane. A sailplane is an aircraft that does not have a motor. It is towed into the sky by a motor-driven airplane until it reaches 2,000 feet or so, when the pilot of the sailplane pulls a lever in his cockpit, releasing the tow rope from the airplane and begins to soar like some giant bird.

There was a time when I talked so much about the joy of soaring that friends would walk the other way when they saw me coming. I was fascinated with the silence of flight without a motor. I took advantage of any and all chances to fly, and so, when One Tank Trips began, one of the first attractions I thought of to show viewers was soaring.

Videographer Jim Holloway and I had driven to Elmira, New York, the cradle of America's soaring industry. This is the hometown of the Schweizer Sailplane Company. It is also the home of the National Soaring Society museum on Harris Hill, overlooking Elmira. An airport on top of the hill offers sailplane rides and instruction, and we had made arrangements for me to take up a sleek new low-winged, high-performance sailplane with an instructor, while Jim would go aloft with the tow plane. After we had cut loose, the tow plane would fly in formation with us so Jim could photograph me at the controls of the sailplane.

The first problem was that the regular pilot was not available for the tow plane, so a retired pilot was contacted and he agreed to fill in. However, when he arrived we began to have a few doubts. He was in his eighties! He had flown during World War II. The instructor assured us that he was well-qualified and pointed out that, besides, he was the only pilot available if we wanted to do the story.

While Jim had a few misgivings, he finally agreed to go with the very senior pilot. They took the door off the plane so Jim could sit in the doorway with his camera while wearing a safety belt, and do some plane-to-plane photography as we flew.

The tow rope was hooked onto our sailplane and, with a wiggle of the tail rudder, I gave the signal that I was ready for takeoff.

We taxied smoothly across the top of the hill. I was already airborne, holding my sailplane about two feet off the ground as the tow plane, still earthbound, bore on towards the end of the runway. Finally, slowly, he lifted off just before the end of the pavement. It was a good thing, because less than a hundred feet beyond the end of the runway was a cliff that dropped off into the Chemung Valley, nearly two thousand feet below.

As we climbed, the umbilical cord connecting us dragged me again and again into the turbulent wake of the power plane. I was very happy when we finally reached an altitude of about 5,000 feet and the instructor told me to disconnect the tow rope.

I pulled the lever and, as I saw the rope drop away, I pushed the stick forward slightly and started to gather some speed to do some wingovers while Jim and the pilot of the plane caught up with us to start taping the action.

I noticed that they had flown back to a spot just overhead and slightly in front of me. I could see Jim, sitting in the open doorway, his legs dangling out of the plane, pointing his camera at me as I moved my stick to the right and gave it full right rudder. I tipped up on one wing and turned away from them. What I didn't see immediately was that the pilot of the tow plane had decided to stay with me, apparently forgetting that Jim was sitting in the open doorway. He performed the same maneuver, with his plane going up on one wing. The movement left Jim Holloway hanging from his belt in the doorway!

As I leveled out I looked above me and was shocked to see Jim's legs churning in empty air. He seemed to be frantically trying to climb back inside the cockpit. A few seconds later he made it, and the plane suddenly veered away from us and started descending towards the airport. The pilot radioed us that Jim had just informed him that he would prefer to shoot the rest of the scenes from the runway, on the ground!

Soaring Society of America
National Museum, Harris Hill
Elmira, New York

(607) 734-3128

Handicapped access: No

TOM AND HUCK WERE HERE

Here's a great trivia question. Were Huckleberry Finn and Tom Sawyer written by Mark Twain in Mississippi, Colorado, or Elmira, New York?

The answer may surprise you, but it was in Elmira, New York that Twain's pen brought to life the antics of Huck and Tom. This was his summer home, where he did much of his writing in an octagon-shaped gazebo on his farm. Today the gazebo is located on the campus of Elmira College and is open to the public. Twain and his family are also buried in this town.

Mark Twain Study   (607) 734-3911
Elmira College
Elmira, New York   Handicapped access: steps into gazebo

STOP AT THE PIG FARM

If you have youngsters, you may want to stop at the pig farm here in the Finger Lakes of Western New York. This is an actual working pig farm that the owners have turned into a tourist attraction. You can tour the barns, hold baby pigs, eat in the cafeteria (barbecued pork—what else?) where "pig cookies" are also served. There are several cartoon characters dressed like pigs and a small gift shop. It's a different sort of place to spend a day.

Misty Meadow Pig Farm   (607) 869-9243
2828 Vineyard Road
Romulus, New York, 14541   Handicapped access: gravel driveways.

A NIGHT IN A PALACE

Paul Newman has stayed here. So have senators, opera stars, and many other celebrities. This is Geneva-On-The-Lake Resort, built to look like a 14th-century Italian palace on the edge of Lake Seneca. The inn offers beauty and tranquillity along with formal box hedges, croquet, and a swimming pool. Inside, rooms range from small suites to a grand suite that overlooks the gardens and lake and includes a living room with wood-burning fireplace, two bedrooms (one with balcony), a four-poster canopied bed, two bathrooms, and a complete kitchen. This is a top-of-the-line resort, and their prices reflect that quality, though they do offer package deals that are affordable for special occasions. For an additional cost they also have a dining room with a gourmet chef.

Geneva-on-the-Lake Resort   (315) 789-7190
1001 Lochland Road, Route 14 South, P.O. Box 929
Geneva, New York 14456   Handicapped access: yes to some rooms (no elevator to upstairs)

A NON-ELECTRIC BED AND BREAKFAST

On the opposite end of the spectrum is Pollywog Holler, a non-electric bed and breakfast that can be found hidden away in the woods. The owner is a sculptor and lets other artists use his woods and land as a place to store their sculptures. It makes for an interesting walk to the cabin. What you get for the night is a bed above a sauna. The bathroom is a privy down the lane. Another interesting feature is the well. They have pumped compressed gas into it, so you can draw a whole bucket full of sparkling water.

The bed and breakfast started out as a rustic hunting cabin, but when the owner had heart problems and decided to retire to a less stressful lifestyle, he decided to turn it into a unique bed and breakfast.

Pollywog Holler Bed and Breakfast   (716) 268-5819
Owners Bill and Barb Castle, R.D.#1
Belmont, New York 14813   Handicapped access: steps to cabin, gravel trails

SPEND A NIGHT IN A LIGHTHOUSE

This is one of the more unusual places we have discovered over the last few years. An actual working, historic lighthouse that you can rent by the night or the week. It's at the eastern end of Lake Ontario, not far from the St. Lawrence Seaway. The lighthouse is on the National Register of Historic Places. What you get is actually the old lighthouse keeper's house in the base of the lighthouse. It's a bit primitive, but it does have running water, bathroom, color television, and enough beds for about eight people. The sunsets here are world-class. Reservations far in advance are a must.

Selkirk Lighthouse   (315) 298-6688 FAX (315) 298-6685
Lighthouse Marina, R.D.#2 Lake Road, P.O. Box 228
Pulaski, New York 13142-0228   Handicapped access: some steps

REAL BEEF ON 'WECK

There's a restaurateur in western New York who is trying to make a roast beef sandwich as popular nationwide as Buffalo Wings.

Charlie the Butcher and his family have been in the meat business for several generations. Now Charlie is branching out with a restaurant, across from the Buffalo airport, where he specializes in that distinctly western–New York sandwich: beef on 'weck.

What is beef on 'weck? It's a slow-cooked round roast of beef, cut thinly and mounded on a freshly baked Kimmelweck roll. (A Kimmelweck roll starts out as a kaiser roll, but a baker in Buffalo by the name of Kimmelweck baked pretzel salt on top and renamed them after himself.)

After the beef is piled high on the Kimmelweck roll, some freshly ground horseradish is spread on the meat and it's ready to serve. If you have never had an authentic beef on 'weck, you have missed a rare treat, especially the way that Charlie the Butcher prepares it.

Charlie the Butcher's Kitchen   (716) 633-8330
1065 Wehrle Drive (at Cuayuga)
Buffalo, New York, 14221   Handicapped access: yes

From My Mailbag...

ATTenTion Neil Zurcher:

My family and I are never going To waTch you on TV again. We drove all The way To The Town where you said The grape fesTival was held and all we found was a dog sleeping in The middle of The sTreeT.

--UpseT in Parma

45 Across the Lake

THERE ARE THREE WAYS to get to Canada: fly, drive, or take the ferry. The Pelee Islander has been a mainstay in international travel for years, running daily during the summer from downtown Sandusky to Pelee Island, Leamington, and Kingsville, Ontario, Canada.

Grant Zalba, who is now news director of WJW-TV, started out as a videographer. He and I were working together when we took our first ride on the Pelee Islander some years back. It turned out to be a trip I don't think either of us will ever forget.

We had gone to Canada to do a week-long series of reports about what was on the opposite side of Lake Erie from Cleveland. In those days, we had only a limited number of radio-equipped newscruisers. It was decided that we would rent a car to drive to Canada instead of taking a company car.

Our week in Canada was enjoyable. We got to meet a lot of nice people, as well as see the sights on the northern coast of Lake Erie. One of the first stories we did was on the dock at Kingsville, Ontario, where we met a Lorain, Ohio man waiting for the ferry. He was carrying a box containing the cremated remains of a friend. He told us the man had spent many summers on Pelee Island and it was his last wish that his ashes be taken to the huge Canadian island and buried there. The man had no living family, and when he died, it appeared that the courts would just have him buried in an old family plot. The friend, remembering the man's wishes, appealed to the court and so, on this beautiful early summer day, was taking his friend to his final resting place in Lake Erie.

On our last evening in Erieau, the tiny vacation community directly across from Cleveland, we filmed a pair of bagpipers from the Chatham Post of the Canadian Legion standing on the rocks on the edge of Lake Erie, piping down the sun. A beautiful sight.

On the final day, we arrived in Leamington to board the Pelee Islander for the ride back to Sandusky. It was a hot, muggy June day. Large cumulonimbus clouds were forming in the west as the boat departed. The ship was packed with early vacationers headed for Pelee Island. Our rental car had been sandwiched between two other cars, on the open part of the deck, by one of the deck hands. In fact, the space was so tight that when we wanted to get something out of the car we had to crawl in and out of the open window, because there was no room to open the doors.

As the first hour passed the weather got worse. Grant and I had not paid much attention to it because we were busy doing interviews with the crew and taking footage of the passengers. A sudden bolt of lightning that struck the water only feet from the boat, and the almost immediate clap of thunder, did get our attention. We headed for the enclosed cabin on the first deck to escape the torrential downpour that followed on the heels of the thunder.

The ferryboat, although a sizable craft, began to toss and pitch as we entered the full fury of a Lake Erie thunderstorm. I had always wondered what it would be like to ride out a storm on the lake. It only took a few minutes for me to decide that I wished I was on the shore instead of on this pitching craft.

In the cabin, passengers were looking worried and pale; many were becoming seasick. Grant went to help a young mother traveling alone with two children, who were both terrified by the storm. I fought my way up the ladder to the pilot house and found many passengers hanging onto the rails on the second deck. The crew confirmed we were in a very strong thunderstorm that was slowing our transit, but they had seen many storms on the lake and didn't appear to be worried. Reassured, I lurched out onto the second deck just in time to see what looked like a large fiery basketball strike the water and then start bouncing towards the ship. About 50 feet away it exploded like a bomb. One crew member told me that was "ball lightning." I decided to go back to the enclosed cabin on the first deck.

It was two hours of howling winds and pounding seas as we pushed our way through a veritable wall of water before finally pulling into Sandusky Bay and reaching the dock. On board, the passengers were mostly a pretty damp and pale-looking lot as they filed off the boat to go through customs. We were still on deck waiting for them to bring off our car when we saw a young crew member walk over to it, open the door, and jump back as a gush of water poured out the door. The storm had nearly filled the auto with water through the window we had left open.

Grant and I sponged as much water as possible off the seats so he could drive it off the boat and through customs, where we learned we had just ridden out a storm that had spawned tornadoes doing some damage in nearby Fremont.

The car? We couldn't turn it in for several days. We left it sitting in the sun with the doors and windows open until it dried out. The folks at Hertz did ask if we had carried some fish in the car.

PELEE ISLAND

If you wish to visit the largest island in Lake Erie, remember that you will be visiting a foreign country. That means you have to go through customs. Usually it's just a matter of a couple of questions about where you were born and where you plan to visit in Canada. But they can, and sometimes do, require proof of citizenship. That means you have to produce a visa or at least a notarized birth certificate proving you were born in the U.S. They will not accept social security cards or drivers' licenses.

As for getting to Peele Island, things haven't changed. There are still only two ways to get there: by boat or by plane. You can arrange a flight at the Sandusky Airport. During summer months, when the ferryboat service is running, you can take advantage of its regular runs to the island. Of course, if you own your own boat you can do what thousands of Ohioans do: drive yourself to Pelee.

There isn't a whole lot to do on the island. There are no major motels, only a couple of small, locally owned ones. Some bed and breakfasts are springing up. There are a few restaurants; sorry, no golden arches. They do have a winery, a small museum, a pheasant farm, and a couple of marinas. Nightlife is almost non-existent. This is a place you come to get away from everything, or to just go fishing.

Here are some spots we visited on our trip:

THE FERRY RUN

The Pelee Islander is still running, but has now been joined on some runs by the JIIMAAN (meaning "Big Canoe"). My only complaint about the service is that they offer no narration as you cross some of the most historic waters of Lake Erie. There isn't even a tape recording telling you where you are, or what happened in this area. Also, there is no coffee shop on the Pelee Islander, only some vending machines. If you can't go more than a couple of hours without a snack or a cup of coffee you might want to bring along a thermos and some sandwiches.

Pelee Island Transportation Company   (519) 724-2115 or (800) 661-2220
Ferryboat service from Sandusky to Pelee Island, Leamington and Kingsville, Ont.
Summer months only for U.S. service.   Handicapped access: yes

BED AND BREAKFAST

We visited a bed and breakfast that sits far back from the two-lane road that runs along the perimeter of Pelee Island. Built in 1875, it was once a stone farmhouse and has now been turned into a quaint place for tourists. The bathrooms are shared. Hosts Becky and Howard Strowbridge accept guests year-round. There is a nice wraparound front porch with lots of easy chairs from which to watch the lake.

Stonehill Bed and Breakfast   (519) 724-2193
West Shore Road
Pelee Island, Ontario, Canada N0R 1M0

AN INN AND RESTAURANT

Another spot to stay on the island is at this collection of buildings on the main road. It also houses one of the better restaurants here.

Anchor & Wheel Inn   (519) 724-2195
North Bay Road
Pelee Island, Ontario, Canada N0R 1M0   Handicapped access: steps into building

ISLAND PHEASANT HUNT

One of the ways the islanders make money is by attracting tourists to their annual pheasant hunt. A game farm, owned by the islanders, raises thousands of pheasants each year to be turned loose across the island in the autumn when an invasion of hunters from the U.S. and Canada arrive to spend money on food and lodging while hunting. The islanders also receive a fee for each pheasant taken by the hunters.

Pelee Island Pheasant Hunt   (519) 724-2931
c/o Township Clerk's Office
Pelee Island, Ontario, Canada N0R 1M0   Handicapped access: gravel paths near cages

For Information

For more information about places to stay and maps of the island, contact the Pelee Island Township Clerk's office.

Pelee Island Township Clerk's Office   519-724-2931
Pelee Island, Ontario, Canada N0R 1M0

46 Over, Under And Through The Falls

One of the wonders of the world, Niagara Falls, is just a One Tank Trip away. It's enough for many people to just stand and look at the falls from the many observation points on both the American and Canadian sides. But if you want to get up close and personal with the falls, there are many ways to do it. The newest, and my favorite, starts not at the falls but farther downstream in the quaint town of Niagara-on-the-Lake, Ontario, Canada. Here you will find a jet-powered boat that takes you up the Niagara river, against a 30-mile-per-hour current, through some of the largest rapids in the world, and into the famed Niagara whirlpool.

For starters, you have to sign a release. They have a very good safety record and have never lost a customer. They supply you with a wool sweater, a two-piece yellow rainsuit, and a lifejacket. They suggest that you bring along a change of clothes. The boat, which resembles an open triple-width speedboat, carries about 40 people on each voyage. The captain of the craft and two crew-members stand behind a Plexiglas shield in the rear of the boat. Before departing you are given a short briefing about the river (one of the fastest-running rivers in the world, even faster than the famed Columbia River of the Northwest), and about the boat (powered by two jet engines, it can produce over 1,100 horsepower as it pushes against the current and can reach speeds of nearly 60 miles per hour when headed back downstream), and a short safety lecture (there are no safety belts in the boat; hang on to the rail in front of you and always do what the captain tells you.) Then, the journey begins.

The first 10 minutes are a high-speed run through the rather placid waters of the Niagara that flow into Lake Ontario. But as the river gorge narrows, the water becomes rougher, until you round a bend and spot white water ahead. The area is known as Devil's Hole, and going upstream through its waves almost brings the powerful boat to a standstill. The boat finally breaks free of the rapids and races onward around another bend, and you suddenly find yourself looking up at the Spanish Aerocars that cross the whirlpool on a slender cable of steel. The whirlpool itself doesn't appear as dangerous from the boat, but the captain only takes you through one of the outer rings. In those few minutes, you get a glimpse at the upper Niagara gorge spewing thundering water into the whirlpool, which has been carved out through eons by water tumbling against the stone banks of the gorge. A few sprays of wave hitting the boat barely get you wet. You have just begun to relax when they start the run back downriver.

As you approach Devil's Hole again, you realize that the waves appear bigger from this direction. Some are as high as 20 feet and the jet boat bores right through them. If you weren't wet before, you are now. It feels like you have run into a wall. A wall of water. The boat is flooded, but pumps quickly empty it. I was warned to keep my mouth shut on the way downriver by the captain. I didn't heed his advice and found myself spitting out great quantities of the Niagara River. After getting immersed by two or three smaller waves, we broke free of the rapids and our speed increased as we hit calmer water.

My teeth began to chatter as speed of the boat diluted the 80-degree summer temperature and I found myself shivering inside my soggy sweater and rain slicker. No matter, I had just taken one of the most thrilling rides of my life and couldn't wait to do it again.

Niagara Whirlpool Jetboat Ride   (416) 468-4800
King George Inn, Box 1215
Niagara-on-the-Lake, Ontario, Canada L0S 120
Handicapped access: steps into boat, no seat belts

HELICOPTER OVER FALLS

Another thrilling way to see Niagara Falls is from the seat of a helicopter hovering over the Horseshoe Falls. You can reserve your seat at the helicopter landing field, which is located near the famous Spanish Aerocars. This ride, like others, is seasonal and only goes when weather permits.

Niagara Helicopters Limited   (416) 357-5672
3731 Victoria Avenue
Niagara Falls, Ontario, Canada L2E 6T2   Handicapped access: steps into aircraft

TUNNEL UNDER THE FALLS

If you want to experience the full force of the waterfalls, go behind them—at Table Rock House. Here you take an elevator down a shaft that leads behind the Horseshoe Falls. This tunnel was once used to feed water from the falls to power the giant electric generators here. It's an awesome sight to stand in a doorway carved from stone and see the tons of water from the falls cascading in front of you.

Table Rock Scenic Tunnels   (416) 356- 2241
Table Rock House, Niagara Parks Commission
Niagara Falls, Ontario, Canada L2E 6T2   Handicapped access: yes

CRUISE TO THE BASE OF THE FALLS

The Maid of the Mist has been operating cruises to the very base of the falls for more than a hundred years. The boats must be built in the gorge, because the river waters are too rough to sail a ship up them. The captains operate in some of the roughest water in the world but have never had a serious accident. In fact, they are called on for rescue service when someone falls or jumps over the falls. Passengers are given plastic parkas to help keep them dry as the ships make their way to about 200 feet from the base of the thundering Horseshoe Falls. The ships only operate during late spring, summer, and early autumn.

The Maid of the Mist   716-284-8897
Tourist Cruises, Prospect Point Park
Niagara Falls, New York

The Cars of One Tank Trips

Many people think the only car I have ever driven in the One Tank Trips series is the little 1959 red-and-white Nash Metropolitan. The fact is, we have only used the Nash since we purchased it in 1989. Prior to that, we used several cars during the first ten years of the series.

We started out in 1980 showing me driving my family car at the time, a 1978 Fort Futura two-door sedan. We quickly realized, however, that we needed some sort of signature vehicle, one that would set the series apart from other reports in the newscast. My friends Bonnie and Bill Cutcher of Brownhelm, Ohio came to the rescue.

The Cutchers have a large collection of cars from the 1930s, '40s and '50s; they offered to let me drive their beautiful green 1948 Chevrolet convertible in the series. We used it a few times each year

in some very nearby trips and shot lots of extra scenes of me driving the car. In all, we used the Chevrolet for two years until we realized that it wasn't really catching on with the viewers.

I had mentioned to Bill Cutcher that one of the first cars I owned, when I was in high school, was a tiny Bantam American, made in Butler, Pennsylvania. A few months later, Bill called me. He had just purchased a restored 1940 Bantam Hollywood Roadster. Would I like to use it in the series?

For the next several years, the little two-toned red roadster, just a bit bigger than the pedal-car I had first driven at age four, became the symbol of One Tank Trips. The car became a big hit with viewers and everyplace I went the first question I was asked was, "Where's your little car?" Problem was, we didn't own the car and, besides, its

25-horsepower motor just couldn't keep up with other traffic on interstate highways. Add to that the fact that it was virtually a museum piece and I spent most of my time while driving it worrying that something might happen to it.

I resolved to get my own special car.

Then, in 1989, I saw an ad in a car magazine for a 1959 Metropolitan. I remembered the little car from my high school days. It had a powerful enough motor for normal highway speeds. Most importantly, the price was what I could afford. I traveled to North Canton and bought the car. At first, it was sort of an ugly duckling—black sidewall tires, black top over a red-and-white body, paint job cracked and peeling in places. Today, after a little work, the car sports a white top, original-style white nylon tires, and a new red-and-white coat of paint. When we do take it on the road with us, we can get upwards of 30 miles per gallon and cruise at 55 miles per hour on the highway.

Because the Nash has become the signature of One Tank Trips, I've had to cut down on the number of times I drive it because I don't want to destroy it. I hope that by driving only in good weather I can make it last and remain a familiar sight in northern Ohio for years to come.

Index

Transcontinental Books
5800 Saint-Denis Street
Suite 900
Montreal, Que. H2S 3L5
Tel.: 514 273-1066
Toll-free 1 800 565-5531
www.livres.transcontinental.ca

Bibliothèque et Archives nationales du Québec and Library and Archives Canada cataloguing in publication

Main entry under title :
The Hockey news top 10
At head of title: The Hockey news.
ISBN 978-0-9877474-7-1

1. Hockey - Reords - North America. 2. National Hockey League - Miscellanea. 3. Hockey players - North America. I. Fraser, Edward, 1978-   . II. Hockey news (Montréal, Québec).
GV847.5.H626 2012   796.962'64097   C2012-941998-2

Project Editor: Edward Fraser
Copy Editing and Proofreading: THN staff
Design (cover and page): Erika Vanderveer

Cover photo credits
Domi: Dave Sandford/Getty Images
Roy: B Bennett/Getty Images
Crosby: Bruce Bennett/Getty Images

Printed in Canada
© Transcontinental Books, 2012
Legal deposit — 3rd quarter 2012
National Library of Quebec
National Library of Canada

We acknowledge the financial support of the Government of Canada through the Canada Book Fund for our publishing activities and the Government of Quebec through the SODEC Tax Credit for our publishing activities.